LOVING FOR LIFE

LOVING FOR LIFE
Your self-help guide to a successful, intimate relationship

Judith A. Sellner, Ph.D.
James G. Sellner, Ph.D.

Self-Counsel Press
(*a division of*)
International Self-Counsel Press Ltd.
Canada   U.S.A.

Printed in Canada

First edition: April, 1986
Second edition: May, 1991

Canadian Cataloguing in Publication Data
Sellner, Judith A., 1945-
    Loving for life

    (Self-counsel psychology series)
    First ed. has title: Between the sexes.
    ISBN 0-88908-960-4

    1. Interpersonal relations.   2. Interpersonal communication.   3. Sex role.
I. Sellner, James G., 1943-   II. Title.   III. Title: Between the sexes.   IV. Series
HM132.S44   1991   158'.2   C91-091093-6

Cover photo by Robert Knight/Image Finders, Vancouver

Self-Counsel Press
(a division of)
International Self-Counsel Press Ltd.
Head and Editorial Office
1481 Charlotte Road
North Vancouver, British Columbia V7J 1H1

U.S. Address
1704 N. State Street
Bellingham, Washington 98225

CONTENTS

PREFACE

This book is based on our involvement in couples counseling and workshops over the last 15 years, our own 29-year relationship, and our training in psychology, philosophy, and relationship counseling. Each year we talk to thousands of women and men about their relationships. This book is a distillation of all these experiences and of in-the-field research.

We would like to begin by introducing ourselves to you through individual statements about who we are and what we bring as human beings to our role as counselors.

Jim Sellner

I am co-authoring this book about the battle of the sexes as a male counselor. I am also an individual, a man, a husband, and a father. As an individual, I experience all the pains and joys that are common to humans. As a man, I see the world from a particular perspective. This perspective affects how I interpret what happens among the three people in my family: Judy, our daughter, and myself. For example, if our income drops off, I immediately assume that it is my responsibility to pick it up. As a husband, I carry the learned cultural bias that a wife's role is to love, honor, and obey. As a father, I am aware that I associate success with career or material wealth, not necessarily with relationships. Accordingly, I tend to worry more about our daughter's school work than about her personal growth.

One of my most significant insights in couples counseling has been the recognition of the high degree of sexual bias in my therapeutic interpretations of the conflicts between couples. Sometimes my bias is slanted toward the woman; at other times, in a form of reverse discrimination, I am prejudiced against the man. Sexual bias works both ways and counselors are not immune to it. This insight — which was clearly pointed out to me many times during my training, and currently by Judy when we work together — has made me aware of my sexist responses, and has taught me to let clients know when my bias has influenced me. Most men appreciate this process, while women often feel relieved that a man will admit bias.

As a male counselor, I am making an honest attempt to understand women. I am aware of how much I don't know or understand. I am aware of the many hypocrisies that permeate men's thinking and how men discriminate against women. In my relationship with Judy I have also learned many of the ways in which women attempt to control men as the price of being discriminated against. This constant and ongoing struggle between men and women is the "battle of the sexes," fought to determine who is in control, who is controlling, who feels controlled, and who should let go of control first.

In this book we don't elaborate on the details of the social background to this battle. Nor do we say much about the functional roles in the household, in childrearing, or in job responsibilities of the future. Instead we focus on the dynamics between women and men in intimate relationships, and how those dynamics can change so that movement is toward love, intimacy, and companionship rather than toward the hostility of adversaries who feel the need to defend themselves from each other.

Judy Sellner

I am an individual, a woman, a wife, and a mother as well as a counselor. As an individual, I face the many choices of a person trying to create a successful life. As a woman, I am painfully aware that women are treated as second-class citizens in this society. This view is tempered by the recognition that we humans — women and men — do not treat each other well, and that men are beginning to realize the price they have paid for their assumed superior position.

As a wife, I still retain some of the old expectations of being economically and emotionally dependent, taken care of by my husband when the going gets rough, and romantically wooed when I am feeling down. These feelings persist even though I have worked as a professional for 26 years and acquired many credentials and achievements along the way. I try to balance three sets of values: those I learned from my mother, those inherent in the modern version of what a woman "should" be, and those that reflect my own inner authentic self.

As a mother, I attempt to teach my daughter what it means to be an individual and a woman because I think her happiness will depend on having a clear sense of herself in a very confused world. I am concerned that she know how to build a relationship and develop her abilities so she can be self-sufficient. The experience of counseling has shown me that men do not understand women, but think that they do. It has also shown me that women do not know the values and life goals that men strive so hard to attain. Both sexes expect the other to be like their own sex. The result is disappointment, disillusionment, and anger.

As a woman counselor, I sometimes feel biased in my perception of women as victims of repressive men. At other times I am biased on behalf of men who devote themselves to wives and families who do not appreciate their efforts. In those cases, the men seem to be the victims. I have reached a much better understanding of men through my relationship with Jim and our work together. I know he is not like me and I no longer expect or want him to be. This realization influences how I see men and women when I work with them. In my work, I continually uncover new biases. When I reveal these biases, the person I'm working with is able to recognize his or her own biases and not be confused by mine or by the biases of others. The result is that that person can develop a new awareness of herself or himself as an individual.

ACKNOWLEDGMENTS

This book could not have been written without the guidance and loving confrontations of Dr. Ben Wong, M.D., F.R.C.P.(c) and Dr. Jock McKeen, M.D.,Lic.Acu. They introduced us to the concepts and experience of love and intimacy in relationships.

Dr. Peter Koestenbaum has had a profound influence in the development and articulation of some of the ideas presented in this book. We are most grateful for what he has taught us about clinical philosophy.

Thank you to all those couples who have had the courage to confront their painful dilemmas in our presence and from whom we have learned so much.

We also want to acknowledge our appreciation of each other for our mutual persistence. Many times in our 24-year-long marriage we've despaired about our relationship, but stayed with it when we wanted to run. We've sometimes lost our feelings of love for each other but never our respect and goodwill. We continue to have our differences but no longer do we try to "change" the other. We appreciate that we've been able to learn how to be ourselves while being in relationship. It has been no small task for either of us.

We dedicate this book to our daughter, Jill, now a grown woman discovering the joys and challenges of relationships between the sexes.

INTRODUCTION

This book is written for women and men interested in having richer, more fulfilling relationships, and for those couples who feel their intimate relationship is troubled, adrift, or otherwise unhappy.

For this second group, the self-counseling approach in this book is presented as a practical alternative to formal relationship or marital counseling. It is designed to develop your knowledge, skills, attitudes, and behavior. Followed conscientiously, the ideas and guidelines presented here can enrich your life.

Yet, just as no single school of psychotherapy can legitimately claim to be a universal cure-all, neither can the self-help approach. If you think about the ideas presented here, try out the suggestions, and complete the activities, but find little improvement in your relationship, you can always consider seeing a professional counselor. Such help, in the form of private counseling or couples workshops, seems warranted to us after attempting a self-directed approach. Even the best and most experienced do-it-yourselfers consult professionals from time to time. The last chapter tells you how to find a counselor who will be the most use to you.

Every relationship has its problems. In our experience, we have found that most relationships have similar problems although each couple's encounters with those problems is unique; some couples feel in control of their difficulties, while others feel controlled by them. And that's the main difference between happy, loving relationships and troubled relationships. In a troubled relationship, one or both of the partners feel they cannot do anything, or refuse to do anything, about their painful dilemmas. In fact, you can, with discipline and effort, learn how to control your problems. That is the underlying principle on which this book is based.

Below are some things to keep in mind as you go through this book:

(a) People of any age can learn from the methods outlined here, although if you apply them early in a relationship, it will be easier. Those couples who have a long history together will require more patience, practice, and motivation.

(b) It takes two people to make a relationship succeed, and these methods work best if both partners are involved. However, you can learn a lot by going through the activities on your own.

(c) Except when you are giving feedback to your partner, keep the emphasis on yourself. No one can make you change, and you can't change your partner. Too many couples take on the task of changing their partners as a life project. It never works. All you'll get is resentment and hostility while wearing yourself out in the process.

(d) When you are giving each other feedback, make sure your partner wants to hear it. It's a good idea to say "I have something to say. Are you willing to listen?" If the answer is "yes," then you know you have permission to go ahead. Your partner is likely to be much more receptive to what you have to say. If the answer is "no," don't say it. It will fall on deaf ears anyway. If the answer is always "no," you will have to decide whether you want to be in that kind of one-way relationship. But before you give up, read the rest of the book carefully. You will learn some things that might help.

(e) Relationships take time. If you're not spending quality time working on your relationship, it won't function. Intimate relationships are like your teeth — if you don't attend to them daily and get periodic check-ups, they'll begin to decay and cause you great pain.

(f) As in any counseling situation, you determine your own growth and rate of change. Feel free to agree or disagree with what we say. Write us a letter telling us so. Our intention is to stimulate your thinking and to get you to experiment with the suggested activities. Make up your own mind, then do what makes sense to you. If it works, congratulate yourself. If it doesn't, try something else.

(g) Read the book slowly. Take turns reading it to your partner or a friend. Get a reading group together to go through it with you. We hope you will have some good experiences along the way: some joyful adventures, a few difficult times, new awarenesses, greater self-acceptance, and deeper love for each other.

(h) Finally, a note on intimacy, which is a word that is often used but seldom understood. Intimacy is the invisible thread that connects one human being to another. It is the willingness to disclose yourself completely. In intimacy, you experience trust, loyalty, and the willingness to make sacrifices. It can be a one-way disclosure, but in mutual intimacy the self-disclosure is returned with sincere appreciation and concern for each other's personal interests. Intimacy is the hallmark of successful, loving relationships. When we use the word intimacy in this book, we mean mutual intimacy.

"How do I know I can do it on my own?" you might well ask. You don't. Many of our colleagues shudder at our faith in people's ability to solve their own problems — especially couples. But doing nothing will keep you exactly where you are now. By trying these methods, you will have a clearer idea of what is going on in your relationship. And you will get as much out of this book as you put into it, which is true of relationship counseling as well.

Note: All of the examples reported in this book are accurate reflections of situations from our own relationship as well as those of our clients. However, in the case of our clients, identifying particulars have been changed to protect confidentiality, and occasionally the situations of two or more couples have been amalgamated into one for a clearer and more effective explanation of the concepts.

1
RELATIONSHIPS IN THE 1990s:
TURMOIL, CONFLICT, AND CONFUSION

Helen and Rob met at an office party in the summer of 1971. A shared belief in a balanced lifestyle and pursuing challenging careers led to a deeply passionate romance. Rob was drawn to Helen's keen sense of integrity and her ability to enjoy life. Helen's attraction for Rob centered on his unwavering sense of purpose, plus his attentiveness and charming ways. Two years later they were married in a romantic wedding in which they exchanged vows they had written themselves.

For a time they were wonderfully happy. But about a year after their marriage, things began to turn sour. Helen was dissatisfied with Rob's constant attention to his work, which left little time for her. Rob was angry at Helen for "bugging" him about starting a family, which he didn't want to do until they were more secure financially. He also resented her "jealousy," as he called it, of his work. Their life deteriorated into repeated rounds of bickering, anger, tears, ultimatums, and slammed doors. A year later they separated in an ugly exchange of hurtful accusations over a confessed affair by Helen.

Helen and Rob's story is not unusual. We all know couples who have gone through variations on the same theme. A recent Harris poll showed that 86% of Americans wanted to have a close relationship. But sustaining such a relationship seems to be a difficult task for many men and women when you consider that approximately 40 to 50% of today's marriages

become tomorrow's divorces. About 75% of those people re-marry, but about 45% of them divorce again. No statistics are available for couples who choose to stay together while being unhappy, dissatisfied, or miserable, but it is our observation that intimate male/female relationships are not very satisfying experiences for the great majority of people.

Why do relationships that promise so much love and excitement at the outset often turn out to be so disappointing and painful? The answer is that *love is not enough*. Satisfying relationships do not simply happen; the ability to create and sustain them has to be learned. Most women and men have not learned how to have a loving, satisfying relationship that endures over time. In today's world it is crucial that couples actively learn how to create loving relationships.

a. CHANGES IN THE SOCIAL RULES

Periodically a business organization will change its operations procedures. When it does, it sends out memos to each employee. If it fails to do so, chaos ensues. Even if the changes are carefully explained and understood, conflicts and misunderstandings still occur. We humans have difficulty adapting to change even under the best of circumstances. When we are not forewarned of change, we become disoriented.

Men and women have not been informed of the changes in the rules that govern how they are supposed to relate to each other. For decades the formula for marriage went like this: two people meet and (hopefully but not necessarily) fall in love; they get married; he goes to work; she stays home; they buy a house; they have children; she raises them; the children leave home; each of the children marries; he retires; and the couple spend the rest of their years together in retired bliss. The few people who didn't follow this formula were prodded back on track with the help of family or friends. Those who resisted were such a small minority that they were tolerated, castigated, or ignored.

In the 1960s the rules began to change drastically, but most people didn't take those changes very seriously and continued to act according to the old rules. The consequence has been that people in relationships in the 1990s are confused, angry, and panicky. In the interest of sanity, love, and peace between the sexes, we present the following new rules for relationships that will help you in the present transition period.

1. Don't believe everything you see, read, or hear

We live in the decade of the media. We are presented with 3-minute snippets of life that sensationalize the ordinary. Newspapers, magazine articles, and books all offer miracle breakthroughs that guarantee health, happiness, wealth, and good sex. Televised 15-second information flashes foster a belief that everyone else is "in" while you're "out." Keep in mind that most of us, like you, are ordinary people trying to do the best we can. Each of us has troubles and joys. There are no guaranteed solutions to life's problems. It is important to judge what is right for you rather than automatically accept the latest fad as the answer.

2. Relationships can take many forms

Traditional marriage is the oldest institution on earth. It serves many purposes: to pass on the family name and traditions, to ensure the protection of property, to legitimize sex between men and women, to produce children, and to provide society with an economic and political unit to keep order. If love and friendship develops in a marriage, that is good. If not, the couple is expected to continue the marriage anyway because its continuance is in the best interests of society. In the traditional view of marriage, personal desires are secondary to the stability of the institution.

In the last 25 years, the basis of marriage and relationships has changed dramatically. Some people still hold the traditional view, but that is now only one option. For the majority of people, love, commitment, companionship, pleasurable sex, equal partnership, and support for personal growth are the primary motivations for being together.

Today's relationships take many forms: marriage, living together, blended families, and intimate acquaintances are a few of the options. There is a significant shift toward personal fulfillment and mutual love rather than toward societal or family obligations. This change requires you to engage in a process of knowing who you are and what you value.

Intimate relationships in the 1990s have become the forum for developing self-awareness while loving another. It is what we call *being yourself while being in relationship*.

3. Women and men have always had and will continue to have problems relating to each other

In the past, problems between the sexes lay hidden beneath the surface of marital obligations. Today they are out in the open. The basis of these problems is that men and women do not understand each other. They see the world through different eyes. They operate on different sets of basic assumptions about life. They will never completely understand each other.

In an intimate relationship, those misunderstandings become clearer and are then acknowledged and accepted. Sometimes a misunderstanding is cleared up and, for a while, both people know they are understood. It is within that kind of environment that you can truly love another and be loved in return. To love another without full understanding requires courage. To see that your partner is at least interested in trying to understand you, in spite of the difficulties, is to experience love. When you know that at least one other person understands you, you can love and allow yourself to be loved. This rule means that to be in relationship requires courage, persistence, and patience. It means giving up the belief of living happily ever after. It means that, over time and with effort, you and your partner can grow to understand each other better and, in doing so, grow old together lovingly and gracefully.

4. The two-paycheck couple has revolutionized male/female relationships

Many women are no longer economically dependent on men. The two-paycheck relationship violates a basic rule of traditional male/female relationships, which says that women's place is in the home. It also violates the rule that assigns to the man the role of being head of the family. Without her paycheck, he would have to drastically alter his lifestyle and aspirations. The roles of wife, husband, mother, lover, father, and breadwinner are blurring. Women and men have become more obviously equal, as symbolized by the great determinant of independence in this society — money.

At the same time, when both partners work, life becomes more complicated. Where there are children, daily chores and commitments must be tightly scheduled into a few weekend and evening hours. Two-paycheck couples often have little time left for each other — even less for themselves. In a childless marriage, one or both partners may concentrate, perhaps for an agreed-upon time period, on a career, while their relationship is given a lower priority. The decision about whether or not to have a child is complicated by economics, expectations, and the lingering pervasiveness of the old rules that were assimilated in a traditional family or educational system.

5. Men will have more difficulties than women adjusting to the new rules

Men have been trained to maintain their poise and self-control and to meet society's performance standards. Males often suppress their complaints until they suffer a breakdown, overextend themselves, ruin their health, or are left by their loved ones. Most men live in a world of self-inflicted isolation, protected by a standardized facade of joviality, superiority, and relentless ambition. All of these characteristics interfere with their ability to be intimate with a woman.

In today's changing relationships, men are in a double bind. They will be ridiculed no matter what position they take. If they live up to society's performance standards (that is, if they are confident, competent, ambitious, and well paid), they will arouse the envy of women and be labeled "macho" — an intended slur, not a compliment. If they reveal their anxieties, weaknesses, and feelings, or ask for maternal compassion from women, or pull back on their career, they will be considered "wimps" by some women, or as "having no balls" by other men. It requires a great deal of courage for a man to have an intimate relationship with a woman that is on his own terms and respects her integrity.

6. A woman must learn how to be an individual with a man while retaining her value of relationship

Historically, women have learned to subordinate their individuality in order to stay in a relationship with a man. Economic necessity was one obvious reason, but a more powerful influence was the socialization that began almost as soon as a woman struggled out of her mother's womb. Even today, many otherwise sophisticated, independent, accomplished women do not feel complete without a man. Others feel like a failure if they have not borne children. A woman's task in a modern relationship is to extricate herself from the limitations of her sex-role conditioning without destroying her capacity to enjoy an intimate, loving relationship. This means she must become more assertive, live according to her values (in spite of the pulls from her partner, her job, her children, or her internal desire to give up the struggle), and learn how to deal with the face-to-face conflict that is part of being in relationship. Paradoxically, a couple's relationship can be a refuge from conflicts if they can learn to mediate the tensions.

7. Success and love in relationships comes to those women and men who rise to meet each day's challenges with creativity and imagination

Anybody can have a successful relationship. It takes knowledge, skills, a positive attitude, and a willingness to risk new behaviors in order to create a loving, fulfilling relationship in which you feel good about yourself and your partner. These four components of successful adaptation to change are discussed in more detail in the next section.

b. THE FOUR KEYS TO ADAPTING TO CHANGE

1. Knowledge

Knowledge is easy to attain. Reading and attending courses or seminars are ways of increasing your knowledge. Creating a successful relationship requires an understanding of the dynamics of relationships. But understanding the concepts is one thing; being able to translate that knowledge into effective behavior is another. Almost every couple knows they should communicate more — it is the single biggest complaint we hear from couples. Once you have the knowledge, you then have to acquire the skills to put that knowledge into action.

2. Skill

A skill is a developed or learned ability to use your knowledge effectively. Two of the key skills required for effective communication are talking clearly and listening. If you want to tell your partner that you love him or her or that you have a problem with his or her behavior, you must convey that message clearly and succinctly. If your partner has the ability and willingness to listen, he or she will understand you. Subsequently you will know if your partner has heard you if you have developed your listening skills.

Competence in a skill occurs over time and with practice. There is no way around this fact. For example, the more time you spend practicing the piano the more skilled you will become. We all envy the person who can sit down at the piano and reel off song after song at a party. We don't see the hours of painstaking work that it took to be able to play that way. The same is true of relationships. There are some basic skills that you must learn and practice on a daily basis if you want to have a successful, loving relationship. Chapters 2 to 8 outline those skills and how you can acquire them.

3. Attitude

An attitude is how you feel, positively or negatively, about what you know. Attitudes are difficult to change because their source is emotional, not rational. Your attitudes are created out of your entire life's experience. For example, if your parents fought a lot when you were growing up, you likely have the attitude that fighting is bad. With this attitude you might avoid fighting at all costs. Whenever a disagreement arises between you and your partner, you'll leave the room or clam up. If your partner doesn't understand this, he or she will probably become even more angry at you. This response, of course, will reinforce your negative attitude about fighting — it's bad! If your parents fought but were able to work through their disagreements, make up, and continue to express their love, then your attitude will be that fighting can be a useful way to resolve differences. You won't be too reluctant to stand your ground.

A negative attitude is one that closes you off from learning. You're not open to change. You can tell when you're expressing a negative attitude when you say "Yes, but...," or "Yes, I know what you're saying, but I'm not going to change my opinion," or "It doesn't matter what you say...." You've closed your mind to discovering something new. Over time this leads to what we might term "psychosclerosis" — hardening of the mind. Like a self-fulfilling prophecy, a negative attitude leads to negative experiences with people. If you think no one will ever love you, you will never experience that love, not because it isn't there but because you're closed to the possibility of it ever happening.

Fear of being hurt physically, emotionally, or spiritually underlies all negative attitudes. When parents fight to hurt each other and there is no forgiveness or resolution, a child hurts. The child forms a negative attitude in order to prevent hurting like that again. It's like pulling up the drawbridge to a castle when it's under siege. The defenses are up and all lines of communication are cut off from the outside world. Anyone who tries to get in is greeted with a frontal attack.

A positive attitude is keeping an open mind; it is the willing suspension of disbelief; it is essential to learning. It is equivalent to saying, "All my experience to date has led me to believe that fighting is bad, but I'm willing to take a risk with you that this time it might turn out differently. I'm trembling in my boots but I'm not going to let that stop me." If you are working toward intimacy, your partner must respond by acknowledging and respecting your fear. As you accumulate more and more positive experiences, you will become more open-minded. You will then be willing to consider another point of view. You will be more willing to risk intimacy. You will develop a positive attitude about your relationship.

4. Behavior

A behavior is the external expression of your desire to have an effect on the world. Behavior is effective if you get what you want. It is ineffective if you fail to get what you want. Altering your behavior is much more difficult than changing your knowledge, or attitudes, or learning new skills. For example, the typical smoker knows that smoking is unhealthy, and most smokers have a positive attitude about quitting. Some smokers even take courses to develop the skills to quit — but they still smoke.

You change your behavior only when you're motivated to do so. Motivation can be internal or external. Lasting, satisfying change in behavior occurs when you are internally motivated. External motivation (sometimes referred to as threat, force, punishment, or coercion) may be effective in the short run, but only internal motivation, or willingness, creates long-term behavioral change.

EXAMPLE

John had a number of affairs over the years. Each time Jill found out, she would threaten to leave, at which point John would promise to be faithful. Jill did leave one time for a two-month period. John entered counseling, gained insights into why he became involved with other women, and learned how to communicate better. Jill returned and John became very supportive and loving. Two years later, John had another affair.

John: I was away on a business trip, got drunk, and went to bed with an associate. Immediately afterward, something snapped inside me. I recognized what I had been doing all those years. I was lying to my wife, betraying my children, and taking the easiest route when the going got tough. I had gone to counseling to please Jill. I learned the right words, but I was only acting. Worst of all, though, I was lying to myself. I knew right then and there I would never have another affair. I can't completely explain it, but I've never wanted to again, and that was 15 years ago.

Knowledge, skills, attitudes, and behaviors are all interconnected. By trying out unfamiliar behaviors, you can acquire new knowledge that will affect your attitudes. Practicing skills can help you acquire new behaviors that will change your attitudes and lead to the discovery of more knowledge. We humans are complex, interesting creatures who have a remarkable capacity for learning, given the proper environment and a willingness to take risks.

2

THE FIVE PERSONALITIES IN RELATIONSHIP

"To thine own self be true," wrote Shakespeare over 300 years ago. We each think of ourselves as having only one self or one personality. In fact, we have many selves. We each have a personality that we exhibit in the workplace, another we show at home, one we see when we are with our parents, and yet another when we are alone. The healthy person is aware and in control of all his or her different personalities and can be the self that is appropriate in any given situation. For example, when you are asking your boss for a raise, you might unthinkingly act like a child pleading for a favor. If, however, you are aware that this is the aspect of yourself that usually emerges when you're afraid, you could choose a more appropriate personality for the situation. Instead, you could act as a responsible adult presenting a legitimate proposal to another adult. If you get the raise, your fun-loving self can emerge as you kick up your heels in celebration.

Each of our personalities has a negative side and a positive side. The positive side of your responsible self is conscientious about your various duties, but the negative side is driven, demanding of others, and harshly critical. When you are under stress or in crisis, your negative self tends to take over and you act as if that is the only self you have. Symptoms such as constant anger, apathy, remoteness, workaholism, defensiveness, emotionalism, and withdrawal indicate that your negative self has taken over. Knowing all those parts of your self that you have available to you at any time — the good, the bad, the ugly, and the beautiful — will help you deal with this situation when it arises.

In a relationship between a woman and a man, there are basically five personalities operating at any given time. First, there is the woman as an individual; second is the man as an individual; third is the woman relating to the man; fourth is the man relating to the woman; and fifth is the "couple's personality," which is the man and woman interacting. Under stress the worst side of each of those personalities emerges and causes problems unless you're aware of what is happening.

EXAMPLE

George: When I'm alone I feel quite capable and calm. I experience this the most when I'm working in my shop. But as soon as Lois walks into the room, I feel myself tense up. She doesn't even have to say anything — it's her presence I react to. I often hear myself criticizing her for any little thing, like not using words correctly. Then, when we get into an argument, it's like I'm another person. I try to be rational, but I find myself getting so frustrated I start yelling and saying things I don't even mean. Then she defends herself and we're like two cats fighting.

Lois: When everyone is gone from the house, I can sit down at the piano and play effortlessly. When George walks in I stop playing and start thinking about what I have to do to make him more comfortable. I can't tolerate any criticism from him. I fall apart. Then I feel like a helpless child. I hate that feeling, so I attack him and the battle is on.

a. PERSONALITIES #1 AND #2: WOMAN AS INDIVIDUAL/MAN AS INDIVIDUAL

You are *born* female or male, but you are *taught* to become a woman or a man. Each man and woman is a unique and special person. No other human can know what it is like to live inside your skin, to see through your eyes, to feel what you feel, to hear with your ears, or to experience what is in your mind. In this respect, no one can completely understand you. You also have a personal history created out of your own unique perspective on your life experiences combined with your experience of the world as a female, a woman, and an individual or as a male, a man, and an individual. This is presented in Figure #1.

The first requirement of a successful relationship is that each person must be recognized and acknowledged as a distinct individual. It is only in a relationship that you can experience your identity. Put another way, you really get to know who are you when confronted by the reality of another. The main purpose of long-term relationships is to discover who you are.

However, one of the underlying assumptions in our society is that love requires you to give up part of your identity in order to "make the relationship work." This assumption is certainly part of the expectations of a traditional marriage. It has had a disastrous effect on both men and women and is one of the main contributing factors to marriage breakdown. It is simply not possible to live a happy, satisfying life when you have sacrificed part of yourself in exchange for another's love.

The idea that self-growth is an important quality of a relationship is highly criticized today and is called self-centered, narcissistic, and selfish. Critics charge that it leads to abusive behavior, alienation, and empty relating. In a relationship without love, those charges are justified. But without mature love, relationships do not make sense anyway.

FIGURE #1

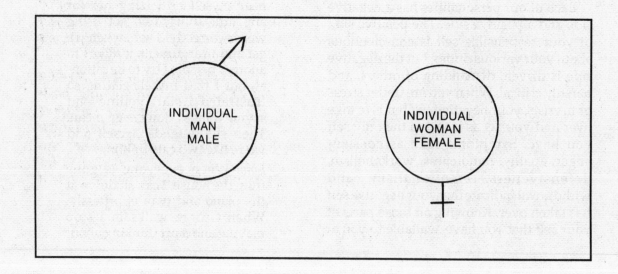

There are four key elements of true or mature love.

    (a) You respect your loved one's individuality. You acknowledge, respect, and accept that your partner is, first and foremost, a person with his or her own likes, dislikes, tastes, opinions, and values. This acceptance means taking pleasure in seeing your loved one achieving happiness on his or her own. You also feel empathetic toward your partner when he or she is in pain, but you don't feel obligated to rescue your partner. One of the most difficult aspects of loving another person is letting go and not interfering with his or her independence.

    (b) Your partner is the one person in your life you value above all else. You do not treat him or her as you treat others. Your partner is someone very special to you and for whom you will go out of your way to show your love. You will do whatever is necessary so that your partner can blossom into an authentic personality.

    (c) You respond to your loved one's needs and concerns even though it may be inconvenient for you.

    (d) You seek knowledge about your partner. You are genuinely interested in learning about your partner and seeing him or her without distortion — warts and all. Your loved one must also be willing to disclose everything to you. The only way a relationship can work is through the movement of two individuals toward developing their capacity for mature love. In the context of a relationship, two unique personalities continually evolve, which ensures that the relationship remains fresh, vital, and alive while two distinct individuals each become more aware of themselves.

b. PERSONALITY #3: A WOMAN'S DILEMMA RELATING TO A MAN

As part of the socialization process, women develop a deeply ingrained attitude that can be expressed as, "Once I have a man who can take care of me, I will not have to be responsible for my own development." There are profound implications in this unstated attitude for both women and men. For one thing, a woman's personality changes in reaction to the presence of a man. He does not have to say or do anything. If you are a woman reading this book, be aware of yourself the next time you enter an elevator in which the only other person is a man who responds to your presence with a friendly smile. Then compare your reaction to when you're in an elevator with a woman who gives you a friendly smile.

The first reaction is shown in Figure #2. The arrow indicates that the woman's attention is directed toward the man as a male and as a man, and away from herself. While reacting this way, the woman loses awareness of herself as an individual and as a female; these aspects become subordinate to herself as woman. She also does not perceive the man's individuality.

Even today, men usually take the lead in initiating relationships, but it's the woman who most often ensures the relationship will continue. She will be the first to seek outside advice, usually from friends or relatives, and she will likely be the one who presses the man to go for counseling if their difficulties reach crisis proportions.

In a troubled relationship, it is generally the woman who is in the "plaintiff" position. She may charge that her partner is indifferent, avoids physical closeness except for sex, doesn't understand her, oppresses her, or is more interested in his work or hobbies than in her. She might complain of a variety of physical and emotional ills, such as nervousness, exhaustion, headaches, or dizziness. She may also feel depressed, moody, uninterested, and even suicidal. These are all symptoms of a female who has given up her individuality for the security of relationship. To outsiders she appears fragile, weak, and in need of help. She complains that she is totally responsible for the care and feeding of the children and has no opportunity to express herself. She often threatens to divorce her partner, which gets his attention for a while. Even while all this is going on she can go to work, competently carry out her duties, and relate well to her co-workers—in other words, play out the role of being a woman in the 1990s.

In relationships with men, women are often afraid of taking control of their individual unique selves. Traditionally, women have been taught to subordinate themselves to the service of others. This dilemma becomes painfully obvious to the vast majority of women who have entered the work world and feel competent and proud on the job, but when they go home at the end of the day, they experience a pressure to give in to the man's desires.

When they do give in, the worst sides of their personalities emerge under the stress and strain of trying to be responsive to a seemingly never-ending list of demands.

Each woman usually begins a relationship expecting intimacy, togetherness, fun times, honesty, compassion, and fidelity. To many women, it is better to have high and unfulfillable expectations of a relationship than to lower those expectations to a mundane, boring level. A woman may persist in her pursuit of those ideals through the most trying times and will seek reinforcement of them through her allies — children, women friends, or relatives. She may badger the man to behave in a way that indicates to her that love is still alive; she perceives any deviation from the ideal as the beginning of the end of the relationship. She may even resort to reading romance novels to maintain the vision of what is possible in a relationship. She sometimes seeks support by becoming ill.

Women often feel they are not taken seriously by men, and indeed their fears are mostly well-founded. Women are disillusioned about intimate relationships more often than men. They may feel betrayed and believe that they invest more

FIGURE #2

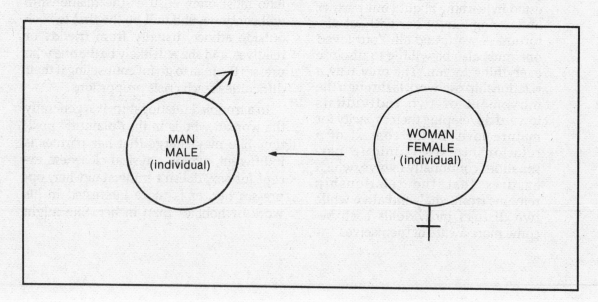

in their relationship than men do. Women expect their personal development and growth to be respected and feel betrayed when men are unsupportive. In desperation, women will use what men consider exaggerated emotional behavior to get a response to their demands.

This type of behavior can be interpreted in a number of ways. The traditional therapeutic approach might be to label the woman as hysterical or (if later in life) as menopausal. The therapist's notes might read something like this: "Mrs. M has a tendency to show theatrical, highly emotionally charged behavior. She uses her emotion to manipulate her husband and she attempts to gain an ally in the therapist. Her suffering and complaining seem to be attempts to blackmail her husband into submission. Her rather feeble calls for help are a further attempt to have things her own way. She is irrational and unrealistic in her complaints, which lack any logic or objectivity and result in regressive and infantile behavior. She has an immature approach to life and expects assistance from her husband and others without the willingness to accept responsibility for her own failure." Drugs might be prescribed to calm this woman down, and she would be given some insight therapy to cure her "neurotic behavior." Her husband would be advised to talk to her more and to be more patient with her. Traditional therapy and traditional marriage go hand in hand.

We would approach such a woman from a very different perspective. Much of her difficulty is because she is very much in touch with her individual values. Her symptoms are messages from her unconscious that she is betraying those values. She is likely much more emotionally developed and open than her husband, and is less satisfied with herself when she lives according to the half-truths of her marriage. She puts more effort into the maintenance of their relationship than her husband does, and she is more responsive

to his wishes because she believes that a relationship is made up of give-and-take. Certainly she feels much pain as a result of her more highly developed emotional expressiveness, but she is apparently healthier than the man. Her ability to show and admit her weaknesses and to seek help turns out, in the long run, to be her strength. Because she "falls apart" under stress, she can regain her balance more easily and is therefore able to survive more difficult crises than her partner. Over and over again in our practice we see women emerge from major life crises more easily than men, who fight to stay in control.

A woman's pain and suffering is often a result of trying to live up to the new image of woman in the 1990s while at the same time submitting to her partner's view of life. Her emotionally exaggerated behavior is often an attempt to pierce the man's emotional unresponsiveness. Because she thinks she is not being taken seriously by him, she decides in desperation that the only way to penetrate his world is with the most powerful weapons she has at hand — her emotions. Following the explosion, after which he may or may not respond to her, she feels exhausted and even more desperate.

This is not to imply that her partner is bad, or wrong. It does mean that if the woman ever wants to have a satisfying relationship, she will have to rediscover that part of her self that is strong, independent, and has opinions. The man's task will be to respond positively to his partner as a person with her own views, likes, and dislikes. If he doesn't respond, she will be faced with a decision to stay or leave, not because she is a failure or emotionally unstable but because she is not getting what she wants in her relationship with this particular man. The results have profound implications for her unique independent self, which will result in her experiencing higher self-esteem and self-respect.

With the rise in the number of working women, many women are choosing another way of dealing with unhappy relationship.

These women become deeply involved in their careers as a way of avoiding their dissatisfaction at home. They borrow part of the male value system and erect a citadel of staunch independence, inaccessibility, cynicism about relationships, and an almost exclusive emphasis on their careers. They occasionally become involved with men, but these relationships usually turn into disasters in which the women, once again, feel hurt and victimized.

Although these women appear to be independent, the focus of their unhappiness is still in the direction of the man, as illustrated in Figure #2.

c. PERSONALITY #4: MEN RELATING TO WOMEN

A man also changes his personality in the presence of a woman. The elevator experiment outlined earlier is helpful for men too. Figure #3 indicates the dynamic. The dotted arrow indicates that the man is emotionally dependent on his partner and in being so loses a sense of himself as an individual and as a male. He does not see her as an individual. Paradoxically, he must maintain his image of what it means to be a "man," that is, independent, strong, rational, and in control.

One of men's greatest fears is the fear of losing control. To be out of control is bad. To be in control is good. Most of men's activities are directed toward gaining, maintaining, and expanding their sphere of control. This is the main reason why men have so much difficulty in their relationships with women. Control is the opposite of intimacy. As a man experiences vulnerability (that is, being out of control) with a woman, he begins to look for ways to get himself back into control. Being an independent personality is one of men's favorite ways of maintaining control. But in a relationship with a woman, the measure of a man's independence is totally dependent on the woman. He can reassert his sense of independence by insisting on his space, being late, hanging out with "the boys," or being secretive. Second, he can demand his partner's approval for any activities he knows she won't approve of,

FIGURE #3

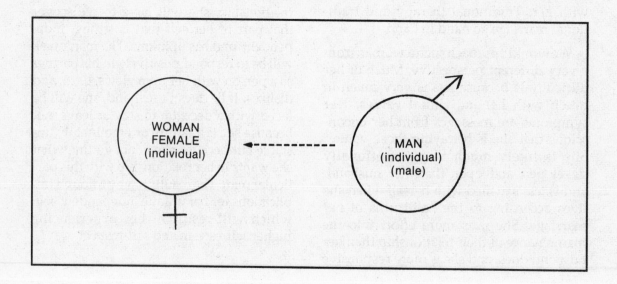

then go ahead and do them anyway. Or, if she does approve, he will lose interest in them.

It is easy to understand, then, why it is so difficult for a man to admit his insecurities and weaknesses. He fears that, if he does expose them, his partner will gain control against him. This is why men do not like to show their feelings and will insist that they can manage their own problems. Additionally, men believe that they should be able to handle any kind of stress without flinching. A man may deal with this by keeping his partner totally under his thumb so that she dare not say or do anything without his approval. He takes charge of all the responsibilities except those he decides can be relegated to her, but she must be watched closely in case she makes a mistake, which he must criticize and correct. Money is the favorite arena for this struggle for control.

Other men attempt to maintain control by tolerating the woman's reproaches or emotional outbursts without batting an eyelid. These men believe they should be able to offer their heads as emotional punching bags to women. They believe that they must be rational in the face of women's irrational outbursts. "Someone has to keep it together — she's always flying off the handle" is a phrase men often use to explain their staunch rationality.

It is a man's tremendous ability to control and suppress his own feelings of anxiety, guilt, and weakness that prevent him from seeing, acknowledging, or accepting the woman's feelings and responding to them. He prides himself on his ability to deal with the woman's "irrational behavior" without losing control. She, however, interprets his imperviousness as arrogance, insensitivity, mental cruelty, and brutishness. Occasionally he might break down in front of her. Then, when he is feeling most vulnerable she will attack him out of revenge and hurt, which further reinforces his belief that to let go of control means bad things will happen.

Men's behavior can be interpreted in a number of ways. Until very recently, traditional approaches to therapy didn't even consider a man's inability to express feelings, develop intimacy, or have satisfying relationships as a sign that he was in need of psychological help. It was usually the woman who was diagnosed as having the mental problem, while the man was gently scolded or given fatherly advice to be more loving with his partner. This traditional approach ignored the evidence that men have a higher incidence than women of serious physical and mental illness. Men have a shorter life expectancy and a higher rate of serious psychosomatic illness, suicide, alcoholism, drunken driving, and violence in general, including wife battering and sexual abuse of their children.

However, most of the male behaviors leading to a life of depression, unhappiness, ill health, and dissatisfaction in love relationships are aspects of the heroic personality expected of men in our society. It is only within the last 10 years that these behaviors have begun to be recognized as unhealthy. As far as relationships are concerned, many men are still resistant to the idea that they have to take responsibility for their part in having created an unhappy relationship.

Men's fear of losing control is complicated by their dependence on women. Statistics indicate that the death rate of divorced men is three times higher than that of divorced women. Mortality rates among widowers six months after the death of their wives is 40% higher than the norm. Coronary failure (a "broken heart") is the single most frequent cause of death in these men. Men are more likely to suffer psychiatric difficulties as a result of divorce than are women. Men will marry much sooner than women following a divorce. Widowers and divorced men are more prone to alcoholism than widows or divorcees. One study showed that the least happy people between the ages of 28 and 32 are unmarried men. Our clinical experience indicates that a man suffers greater upset and has more difficulty getting over the hurt when his partner has an affair than when the reverse occurs. Most men go to great lengths to cover any signs of dependence on their partners for fear of being dominated.

From this perspective, it is easy to understand why men resist reading books about relationships, talking openly about their troubles with their partners, or going to couples counseling. From a man's point of view, these activities just stir up more feelings (which are out of his control as it is) and may uncover his dependence on his partner. To a man, such actions would be like flinging open the floodgates when the river is already lapping over the top of the dikes. Women's enthusiasm for these activities only serves to fuel men's defensiveness.

It is a very courageous and healthy man who will set aside his fears, enter into the process of honestly examining himself, and begin to actively take responsibility for himself in a relationship. But the payoffs are many.

(a) The man can establish an equal relationship with a woman, which will help him let go of his assumption that he must constantly carry the heavy burden of responsibility on his shoulders.

(b) He will develop a greater understanding of himself, and thereby increase his sense of being in control of his life while decreasing his need to control those around him.

(c) If children are involved, he will find a joy in actively participating in raising them, which will add to his sense of significance in the overall scheme of things.

(d) He will be respected and loved by his partner, which will enhance his sense of self-esteem and power as well as increase his sexual fulfillment.

(e) He will gain the insights and skills that will make him a more effective person in his chosen line of work.

It is only recently that organizations have begun to value employees who can deal effectively with people. The best place to learn that skill is in your intimate relationship. If you learn to handle interpersonal problems at home, human problems in the workplace become child's play.

d. PERSONALITY #5: THE COUPLE'S INTERACTIONAL PERSONALITY

When they have to interact with their partners, some of the nicest individuals begin to exhibit their most negative aspects. This situation is represented in Figure #4. The overlapping circles indicate mutual unhealthy dependence between the man and the woman. The arrows show how highly reactive they are to each other and the action is two-way. The parentheses indicate that, in relationship, they don't know who they are — each self is hidden.

Each person feels the need to attack and at the same time to protect himself or herself. The woman will attack using all the so-called "feminine wiles" that she learned while becoming a woman. She sees a need to protect her identity as an individual from the man's onslaught. In the process and over time, she loses touch with her female sexuality. This inner split is often manifested as loss of interest in sex, but sometimes it emerges as promiscuity as a way of gaining relief from the battle.

The man, too, attacks from his learned definition of what is means to "be a man." He is also protecting his identity. His male sexuality suffers in any number of ways.

14

The effect can be sexual dysfunctions such as premature ejaculation, impotence, obsession with sex if his partner won't cooperate, or lack of interest in sex if she's pushing for it. He too may become promiscuous as he seeks relief.

When a couple is engaged in the battle of the sexes, they are like two boxers in the ring carrying on a never-ending match. They are prohibited from knocking each other out because each is dependent on the other for the fight. They have unspoken agreements about breaks between rounds so they can rest. Sometimes they get so exhausted they have to lean on one another for support. At times it is hard to tell whether they are fighting or engaged in an erotic dance. Each will alternate between the offense and the defense. There is no referee in this match — the couple relies on unwritten rules to conduct the struggle. Intermittently, as a reaction to exhaustion or because of a fear that the other partner is about to go down for the count, one partner will break a rule that will bring on a concerted frontal attack by the other, fuelled by angry indignation. Both partners also justify the fight in their heads and gain some self-righteous strength to continue — like a partisan crowd booing

your opponent and giving the "okay" to strike again. Friends, relatives, or counselors may be encouraged to join in by cheering for one of the corners.

From an outsider's perspective, it is easy to come to the conclusion that one partner dominates the other. It is not unusual for one partner to protest the domination of the other to friends, relatives, or anyone else who will listen. A closer examination of the situation will reveal that it is difficult to say who is dominating whom. Often the seemingly passive partner guides and manipulates the actions of the more dominant partner. The passive one decides, while the dominant person executes the decision. For example, if the man is the one with a career, the woman realizes a sense of equal worth as adviser in his advancement, or as a support from which he draws the strength to carry on. In feeling indispensable to her partner's career, she can identify with his success. By relying on his wife to carry on the household and family duties, the man is free to devote his complete attention to the attainment of external success while maintaining the image of being the stable family man. In this situation, the couple's behavior is essential to their unspoken agreement to pursue

FIGURE #4

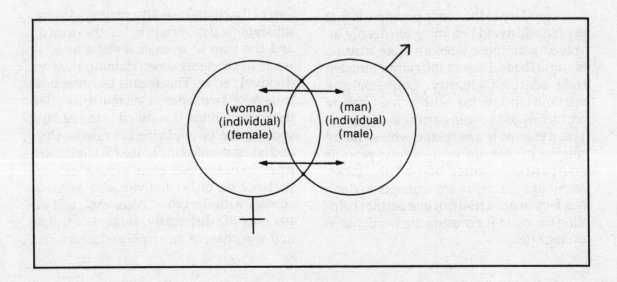

material success at any cost. The issue of who is dominant and who is passive is irrelevant.

The balance of power is intuitively maintained in partner choice, leading to the principle that people who get involved beyond the superficial edges of a relationship are of equal maturity and self-esteem. We have a sophisticated built-in radar system that we use to gain extensive insight into a prospective companion almost as soon as we meet. The initial conversations will confirm or deny those first impressions and help us to decide whether or not to proceed. Each individual has his or her own particular areas of high self-esteem and maturity, but on balance an equal match is formed. For example, a distinguished older man becomes involved with a young, maternal, earth woman because her warm, supportive nature counterbalances his inability to take care of himself. Her fight to become distinguished and secure is offset by his willingness to give her instant security and status. A sense of self-esteem can be gained through various attributes of one's partner, such as intelligence, strength, beauty, and wealth, as well as through personal maturity and the willingness to support and affirm the partner. These qualities, of course, have as much importance as the partner attributes to them.

A corollary to the above principle is that people will avoid becoming too deeply involved with those who are more mature, because the feelings of inferiority threaten their sense of identity. Conversely, a relationship created with a less mature partner would remain narrow and limited. This dynamic is one reason why so many couples run into difficulty in later years as one partner matures beyond the other. Many of their fights are attempts to deny this fact, or are a result of one partner belittling the other for causing the relationship to stagnate.

However, if people of unequal maturity do begin a relationship, a process of mutual adjustment begins. The mature person will try to avoid any accusations of superiority through grand gestures of modesty, humility, and self-depreciation, while narrowing his or her interests and indulging in over-blown praise of the partner's achievements. All these strategies are designed to obscure the reality of the relationship for fear of losing the other. Meanwhile, the less mature partner will be on the lookout for any flaws in the other's character and will generously point them out in order to bring the other down to his or her level.

In the struggle to preserve the balance, each individual's identity is absorbed into the personality of the couple. Over time, when the couple is in contact, each partner's sense of what it means to be a man or a woman is lost. As they lose sight of these aspects of themselves, they begin to feel a loss of personal power when they are interacting. They then feel the need to defend themselves against what they see as an attack by the other. If they allow themselves to be overwhelmed, they risk losing their identity and their self-definition of womanhood or manhood.

e. BEING YOURSELF WHILE BEING IN A RELATIONSHIP

One of the central tasks in creating a loving, satisfying relationship is for the woman and the man to overcome self-alienation while at the same time retaining their individual selves. This means learning how to develop two separate yet mutually relating personalities. It is called learning how to be yourself while being in a relationship, and is represented in Figure #5. The broken lines indicate that each person can experience his or her individuality when in contact with the other. Also, each will experience life differently, either as a female and a woman, or as a male and a man. Yet a connection exists too; they can sometimes choose to be dependent on each other.

The above relationship is clearly differentiated from any other two-person relationships either partner may have. It's like a *pas de deux* in ballet in which the dancers are skilled individuals who, while dancing together, produce something beyond what each could do alone.

When you are being yourself in a relationship, you are conscious of yourself as a member of a couple. You take time to be with your partner, and also to have a life of your own. Your relationship is the one place where you can discuss anything and reveal all that you know about yourself without being punished, ridiculed, or preached at. Within this framework you retain your unique personality (as a woman or as a man), respect the other's individuality, and accept your sex differences. You have clear boundaries not only between yourself and your partner, but also among friends, parents, and children.

Couples often allow their friendships to interfere with the privacy of their intimate relating. If friends can drop in at any time or are told things that should be said only to your partner, then intimacy is compromised. The relationship with your partner should have priority over the relationship to your parents. Parents often have difficulty accepting an adult child's independence; they must realize that in a quarrel their son or daughter will be loyal to the partner, not to them. The wise parent respects this priority; the mature child acts on it.

Children also need to be aware that their parents' relationship is clearly different from and primary to the parent-child relationship. When this principle is respected, the child will feel safe in the family and will not feel forced to choose between one parent or the other in times of conflict. Because opposing camps have not been formed, it will be clear to the child that a fight between mom and dad does not involve the child. The child is then free to observe and learn important interpersonal skills from the fights, knowing that his or her well-being is not at stake.

When you are yourself in a relationship, the outer boundaries of your relationship will not be too rigid. You will be willing to invite others into your life to discuss your

FIGURE #5

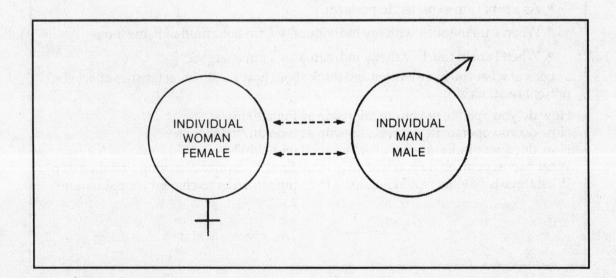

problems, to celebrate the good times, and to ask for comfort or advice during the bad times. You will also be open to helping others in their times of need. With parents and family you will be able to accept them as people who have their own unique characteristics and foibles. Instead of being sources of conflict between you and your partner, they are people to be loved and from whom you can gain an understanding of how you have created your own personality. A sense of balance is the key.

The remaining chapters are designed to help you increase your knowledge and skills and enhance your attitudes and behaviors, so that by being yourself while in a relationship you will feel more in touch with your true self, more able to love, and more open to allowing yourself to be loved. Before reading on, try the first activity.

ACTIVITY #1
WHO AM I IN RELATIONSHIP?

Take three sheets of paper. At the top of one sheet write, "As a *female/male* I am..." Complete the sentence as many times as you can. At the top of the second sheet of paper write, "As a *woman/man* I am..." Fill the page. Head the third sheet of paper with, "When I am in touch with my individuality, I ..." Complete that sentence as many times as you can. Share your statements with your partner.

Here are some examples to help you get started:

- As a *female* I am not safe at night on the streets.
- As a *female* I am aware of my monthly cycles.
- As a *male* I am physically stronger than most females.
- As a *male* I can experience sexual impotence.
- As a *woman* I should be aware of my appearance.
- As a *woman* I have learned to nurture.
- As a *man* I should help women.
- As a *man* I am expected to perform.
- When I am in touch with my individuality I am not afraid of being alone.
- When I am in touch with my individuality I am energetic.

Look at what you have written and think about how these characteristics affect your present relationship.

How do you operate in your relationship as female/male?
How do you operate in your relationship as woman/man?
How does your individuality affect your relationship?
What part of yourself do you tend to give up for the security of having a relationship?
What three behaviors would you have to change in order to change your situation?

3
THE SIX STAGES OF RELATIONSHIP

You see him across the room. You feel a slight shudder, a little shaking in your knees. Almost against your will, your right hand rises up to check that your hair is in place. Your stomach feels queasy. Automatically your other body and mind functions swing into action as your pulse quickens and your chest tightens. A transformation sweeps over you as you assume a hopefully sophisticated, subliminally seductive posture. Your eyes soften; your mind races through the phrases and actions that you have at your disposal to get his attention. He responds with just the right amount of attention, not cloddish, school-boy insensitivity. He exudes a sureness that is compelling, not cocky. You have just "Fallen in Love." Another romance has blossomed as you embark, once again, on the rocky road of relationship. However, the chances of it surviving longer than three years are not great. Although romance makes for a wonderful beginning to a relationship it quickly fades when the realities of trying to make love last create seemingly insurmountable problems between the sexes.

We arrived at this conclusion as a result of our 29 years of personal and professional experiences together. We met in a romantic "boy-meets-girl" fashion in the early 1960s. We were married in 1967 in a very traditional church ceremony with our friends and families gathered around us. We spent the first several years of our relationship doing the usual things people do in a traditional marriage. We finished our university degrees. Judy became a teacher; Jim began a career in city planning. We travelled with friends. We had a child, bought a house, and were doing all the things that we thought we should, with a dose of mandatory experimentation that was expected of young people in the late 1960s. According to the script, we should have been very happy. In reality, we weren't. Even though to our friends we had the perfect relationship, we were, in fact, miserable together.

While attempting to do everything "right," our relationship had become both boring and full of conflict. We didn't really know why and we didn't know what to do about it. The usual patterns developed: Jim got overly involved in his career; Judy devoted more and more time to her daughter; Jim felt left out. A succession of clandestine affairs added to the increasing alienation. In 1975, in a painful crisis, we separated, sold our house, quit our jobs and, in what now seems to be a desperate attempt to understand what was going on, we both began our masters degrees in humanistic psychology. Our relationship and the difficulties we were having became the focal point of our two-year-long studies. A year after we separated we decided to try again, to see if we could be ourselves while being in relationship with each other. We discovered that one of the keys to creating successful relationships lies in understanding that relationships go through six natural, predictable stages and in possessing the skills for navigating those stages.

a. THE ROMANTIC STAGE

First comes the romantic stage. It's wonderful. It's exciting. It's crazy. All your life you've been searching for the one person who will ensure that you'll live "happily ever after," freeing you from the pain, anguish, and strife you encounter in the world.

Falling in love can hit you like a thunderbolt or slowly blossom over months, even years. It can hit you like a ton of bricks or you can feel its warmth gently soothe your body like the morning sun in late spring. However it occurs, the romantic stage holds out the promise of the perfect relationship in which you hope to find a replacement for everything you don't have and don't like about your life. The more you feel you don't have, the more you don't like about yourself, the harder you fall.

For women, these expectations have been fed since birth by a diet of Prince Valiants and Supermen. Men have been made ripe for the picking on a menu of Snow Whites, Cinderellas, and nameless Playgirls.

Before you protest that you are above such silly trivialities, take a look at how your relationships have worked out over the last few years. Have you raised your hopes up only to be dashed by a woman or man who was "too much of this or not enough of that?" Or do you protect yourself from the ravages of love by cynically remaining above it? If so, then you've probably been hurt by love. If it has been a long time since you experienced the senseless abandonment of romantic love you may scoff at the foolishness of it. However, there is not a man or woman who is immune, under the right circumstances or at the right time, to the feverish disease of falling in love.

One of the key ingredients in a long-term loving relationship is passion. Passion brings excitement to relationship. You experience passion when you risk involvement. You get deeply involved with people and in things over which you feel excited. When you're excited about someone you know it will last forever and you make plans. Without passion, you can take it or leave it.

When you fall in love you have the feeling that someone in this world has finally taken notice of you, cares about you, and is interested in you, just because you are you. Romantic love can be fueled by physical attraction, common career goals, shared recreational interests, or personal crises. It will eventually move into the sexual realm because, at this stage, the sexual encounter is experienced as the ultimate expression of oneness. Out of this comes the feeling that your life has purpose and meaning.

To make love blossom you have to risk opening yourself up to the other person. You have to be willing to let go of your independence and allow yourself to be dependent. It's a wonderful feeling. You feel safe. You can take a break from life's difficulties. It is in this atmosphere that you have long intimate talks. You can discuss anything. Each of you finds the other intensely intriguing. You want to know all and tell all.

In romantic love you form a strong bond that can pull you through the trials and tribulations that are part of any long-term relationship. It's a feeling that you were made for each other or that you seem to have found something that has drawn you together.

The romantic stage of a relationship is important and healthy, and it is at this stage that a couple can begin to create a future. However, romance is getting a lot of bad press these days. In the epidemic of failed relationships people are becoming disheartened about love at first sight. Cynics call it an illusion; the more analytical label it as infantile; some say it's a sickness. But trying to put down love is like attempting to hold back the tides. Romantic love can be the beginning of a beautifully creative experience, one that awakens a sense of being alive and adds a sparkle of color and clarity to our otherwise pedestrian lives. It can be the confirmation that your spirit is still alive and living inside. As with any creative act you must possess skills and be prepared to do the work required to transform the vision into reality. It won't happen by itself.

Our capacity to enjoy for its own sake the pleasure that romantic love can provide is very limited indeed. One of the cruelest and most tragic myths in our society is that "love conquers all." It is this myth that creates the belief that romance is the highest mode of personal fulfillment. It leads to the assumption that romantic love must be institutionalized into marriage or formalized into a permanent arrangement of living together. The myth of romantic love can make the most responsible, clear-thinking woman give up responsibility for herself and her future to her partner. The most rational, hard-thinking man gets locked into the belief that his new bride or live-in will launder his socks and be his sexual service station. The myth of love results in the mistaken notion that if you have problems you shouldn't talk about them, because time and love will cure all. This belief inevitably leads to dissatisfaction, resentment, and the breakdown of relationships.

In an attempt to prevent the inevitable heartache that accompanies the myth of "love conquers all," marriage counselors, therapists, and advice columnists have attempted to inject a huge dose of rationality into people's beliefs about romantic love. But what the rationalists don't realize is that romantic love is an irrational affair. It is the antithesis of rationality. Any attempt to rationalize romantic love will be ignored or result in a mechanized, therapeutically obsessive, Woody Allen approach to love and relationships.

Romantic love can only be experienced. There are no skills or answers that will help lovers get through it. One of the thrills of falling in love is that there are no answers. No controls will work; each couple sees their experience as unique. Nothing can be predicted and no obstacle is too large; only possibilities exist. Out of the passion of romance comes the urgency to make it last forever. It sets the scene for the next stage.

b. THE EARLY COMMITMENT STAGE

Each of us carries deep personal desires that we long to fulfill. We want to be loved, cared for, to share life with a special person, to be treated as special.

At the romantic stage you can dare to hope that it will all come true. At the early commitment stage you begin to create the structure for making it happen. You and your partner each begin to ask, "Why are we together?" Questions like, "Shall we move in together?" or "Will you marry me?" reflect the desire to find something permanent around which you can begin to build your dreams. The main quality of this stage is that you disclose a bit more of yourself. You reveal some of your hopes and fears, a few of your foibles, more of your personal history. You introduce each other to your circle of friends and to the scrutiny of the family.

When you answer the question, "Why are we together?" you take the first small step toward commitment. It's like accepting an offer of employment. You have some idea of what you're getting into but your decision is based on high expectations and incomplete information. You are risking your freedom for the security of relationship. It is a risk that must be taken if you ever hope to have a truly intimate relationship. The only way to find out is to jump into the unknown.

People who decide to get married at this stage usually make a commitment to the institution of marriage, not to the love partner. This is particularly true in a traditional marriage in which couples tie the knot before they get to know each other well. This type of couple assumes that, over time, it will all "work out." We think that couples who get married without at least 10 hours of premarital counseling are making the commitment to the institution of marriage rather than a commitment to each other. In essence, they are making a bad contract because they have not negotiated the terms or conditions of their relationship or agreed on the required actions when things go wrong or when conditions change.

Before the 1960s, the institution of marriage was so strong couples endured great pain and suffering in order to preserve the marriage. Today's high divorce rate is witness to women and men being less willing to sacrifice themselves to the institution.

c. THE CONFLICT/POWER STRUGGLE STAGE

The conflict/power struggle stage begins when you realize that your partner is not all he or she is cracked up to be. He does something you don't like. She disappoints or betrays you. You realize that one of your basic values runs counter to hers or his. Your likes and dislikes begin to clash.

Anger, pouting, silence, jealousy, yelling at one another, slamming doors, being late for appointments, not showing up, running marathons, always doing things with other couples, withholding sex, demanding sex, being "nice," feeling tired as soon as he walks in the door, and fighting over money are some of the symptoms of the power struggle stage. Each couple has its favorite syndrome.

1. Falling out of love

Conflicts and power struggles develop because you are now getting into the serious

ACTIVITY #2
REFLECTION

Think about your current relationship or one in which, as an adult, you fell passionately in love with someone.

- How did you meet?
- Was it an immediate attraction or did it develop over time?
- What were the particular qualities of the person that attracted you to him or her?
- Was sex a part of the excitement?
- Are you still with him or her?
- If so, is the romance still there?
- If not, what has happened?
- How has that experience influenced the way you view relationships?
- What do you hope for from a relationship now?
- What are your feelings about romantic experiences?

business of relationship. You've invested a lot of your time and love based on certain expectations. Each of you is starting to disclose more of who you really are. During the romantic stage each of you was putting your best foot forward in order to make yourself attractive. You might have seen a few things you didn't like but you let them go by. In this stage you see negative aspects of your partner that hit you at your core. They tear at you in the tensions of everyday living. The romance has faded; you have fallen out of love.

Conflict is the arena in which you begin to work out the ways and means by which each of you can be two individuals while being part of a relationship. Your individual identities and values emerge. You see some of what you like and much that you don't like. Power struggles arise when he tries to tell you how you "should" be, but aren't and you do the same to him.

You were attracted to each other at the romantic stage for very particular reasons. In the power struggle stage those same things will drive you nuts. You used to talk for hours and he listened intently to your every word; now he says, "You talk too much!" He won't say this directly. He'll read the paper while you're talking to him, or he'll sneak a gaze at the lithe young thing that just passed by. You will get angry. At the romantic stage you loved how he would listen to you for hours. When you're in conflict you say, "Why don't you contribute something to this conversation? I have to do all the talking. I feel like I don't know you any more! Talk to me!"

During the romantic stage he was the mature, competent person who was well established and recognized in the world. At the conflict/power struggle stage he, in your eyes, becomes a tyrant, overbearing and domineering, always offering advice with little time for you because he's so involved with his career. You, who supported and showed excitement about his career, are now degraded publicly by him because he thinks you lack ambition and direction in your life. Each of you begins to hate the differences you once loved.

EXAMPLE

Allison and Jim lived together for a year before they got married. A few months after the wedding Jim became more involved in his work. Allison began to feel cut off and isolated. She missed the closer intimate exchange they had before they married. She withdrew sexually. First, he angrily tried to make her feel guilty, but then withdrew more into his work. He started taking evening courses to further his career. He seemed to have no interest in doing things with Allison. She felt hurt and angry. She, too, began to put more energy into her career. The little time they did spend together was marked by exhausting, hurtful fights punctuated by long periods of silence.

2. Sex and love as bargaining chips

What happened to Jim and Allison? Jim's initial attraction to Allison was sexual, but she was also the "first woman he had met with whom he could talk about anything." Now, from his point of view, she was sexually cold. Their conversations had turned into circular arguments. His blaming statement would be "No Sex, No Love!"

When they first met, Allison was sexually attracted to Jim but more importantly he treated her as an equal and appreciated her emotional openness. Now Jim was emotionally withdrawn and severely critical of her. She took the stance of "No Love, No Sex!" Together they have reached a stalemate, each believing in his or her right to put a hold on the partner to get what he or she "deserves." Both are miserable.

This stage of a relationship is inevitable and unavoidable. It's the stage at which couples separate, divorce, beat each other verbally or physically and enter counseling. But the problem is not that conflicts and power struggles occur in relationships; the problem is that we are not taught how to deal with them and move beyond them. Indeed, long-term love and intimacy is built on a foundation of resolved conflicts and power struggles. Lasting love and deep happiness must be earned. The major difference between a relationship that is chronically and destructively in conflict and one in which love, intimacy, respect and companionship grows is *each* person's willingness to learn the required knowledge, attitudes, skills, and behavior.

3. Fourteen seconds to maximum misunderstandings

The most important skill required for successfully navigating the troubled waters of the conflict/power struggle stage is listening with positive regard. *Listening* means actively hearing and understanding what another is saying. It means paying attention to the words and feelings that are being conveyed. *Positive regard* is respect, empathy, and interest in the other person's well-being. It also means that you have to be willing to openly disclose your thoughts and feelings to your partner. People are always sending out messages about how they're feeling. Most of them are easy to read if you open your eyes, tune in your ears, and close your mouth for a little while. Listening with positive regard is the basic ingredient to creating goodwill between people.

People in conflict do not listen well. We have been studying couples in conflict in our private practice and in couples workshops for the last 11 years. We have found that couples in conflict can listen to each other for a maximum of 14 seconds. After 14 seconds they interrupt, prepare counterarguments, get angry, start yelling, walk away, and do anything but listen. This is the main reason why couples' arguments go around in circles. They don't know what they're fighting about because they don't listen.

Listening with positive regard was one of the first skills that Allison and Jim learned in their counseling sessions. Jim discovered how afraid he was of the emotional dependence he felt with Allison. It was a fear amplified by his history of family violence and divorce. Allison offered emotional contact but Jim protected himself from it by becoming aloof during their conflicts. He wanted to be close to Allison but was afraid that if he let himself become dependent, she would leave him and he would be deeply hurt.

Allison was completely surprised by all of this because Jim had maintained such an air of independence. Jim acknowledged that his independence was a protection against ever being hurt by anyone. Jim's task in counseling was to recognize and accept his vulnerability. He had to risk telling Allison that he felt he could not live without her and to tell her about that. Intellectually he knew he could live without her, but it was his unacknowledged, unexpressed feelings that led to his ineffective behavior. She could then understand Jim's behavior and with his consent, she could begin to confront him whenever he became critical and distant.

Allison, in the listening activity, realized how important it was to her that Jim listen to her. It was, in her mind, a sign that he respected her. Respect was something that was totally lacking in her family. Her mother and father were highly critical of her trespasses while at the same time unresponsive to her accomplishments. She talked about how sometimes she felt like she was going crazy in that environment. She had to face how unloved and unlovable she felt and how she interpreted Jim's behavior in these terms. When Jim was acting aloof she felt totally separated and unable to make contact with him. She felt miserably alone at those times. She learned to recognize when those feelings were beginning to surface and tell Jim about them. Her task was to let Jim love her and open herself to his love both emotionally and sexually.

In conflicts and power struggles each partner defends against the pain and fear of being vulnerable. Each person feels attacked and blamed; each blames and attacks. To move beyond the power struggle you must recognize and reveal what it is that you think you have to protect and then risk not protecting yourself as much with your partner. This, of course, is the meaning of vulnerability — to remain open when the urge is to protect and defend. It is as difficult as it is necessary. An atmosphere of trust and goodwill is crucial. Listening with positive regard is the way to build it.

In our experience, the couples who have been able to do this are those who have retained a memory of the romantic stage. Even those couples who experience the most conflict will stay together and try to make the relationship work under the most "impossible" conditions if they retain that memory. To the outsider it may appear to be an unhealthy dependency, even pathological. But when we ask those couples, "Why in heaven's name do you stay together?" their answer is often, "We have so much going for us at times our relationship is just like it was when we first met." Jim and Allison recaptured their early romantic feelings through their honest disclosure of feelings and desires and by their mutual interest in making the necessary changes in their behavior.

Sometimes the love connection becomes completely lost through years of bitter, hurtful, spiteful, angry conflicts. In these situations you would be better off to let go and move on in your life. This involves moving out of a familiar, predictable relationship, and taking the risk to leave. You can never know what the *right* move is until you experience the results of having taken the risk. For many people it requires as much courage to leave an unhappy relationship as it does to stay and begin to work things out. No one can ever ethically tell you what the right decision is; to do so would be to rob you of your dignity, courage, and sense of identity. You are the arbiter of your life and only you have the authority to judge what is right for you based on your interpretation of the facts and what you want in a relationship.

4. Learning how to listen with positive regard

We have taught thousands of couples to listen with positive regard. They learn how to slice through their conflicts very quickly. With about 10 minutes of practice, you can increase your listening skills by 400%.

Here's how to do it.

Begin by reading the following guidelines. These are the basic ground rules for listening with positive regard.

(a) One person talk at a time.

(b) You don't have to agree — go for understanding.

(c) Do this in a spirit of positive regard.

(d) After you've practiced a couple of times on a pleasurable topic, pick a topic over which you have a bit of conflict. As your listening skills grow, introduce topics that rouse more conflict.

Using this step-by-step approach you will gain competence, confidence, and trust in each other. Your communications will change from angry, hurtful exchanges to scintillating conversations.

Now go on to the next activity to put into practice what you have just learned.

You will likely feel very awkward doing this activity the first few times. With practice, you'll begin to feel more comfortable. Remember to observe the four guidelines.

5. Blowing your cover

When couples are engaged in conflict/power struggles, they are usually trying to control one another. We all have our favorite ways of trying to control people; either directly or indirectly we try to get them to do what we think they should do so we can feel secure. A desire for control stems from a fear that we will be taken advantage of, made to look stupid, or be hurt. The desire for control has a sound basis; somewhere along the way people have taken advantage of us, made us look dumb, and hurt us. The control, however, is a roadblock to intimacy.

EXAMPLE

Allison tried to control Jim by withdrawing sexually from him because she knew that sex was something he wanted. Her thought, of which she was unaware at the time, was, "He treated me well and I felt close to him when our sex life was good so maybe if I withdraw sexually he'll be nice and move closer to me. If he does this I'll reward him with some good sex." Allison's attempt to control didn't get her what she wanted all the time, but it was effective enough to keep Jim from leaving her. She was miserable but at least she wasn't abandoned.

Jim tried to control Allison by becoming staunchly independent and involved in his career. He knew that she wanted him to be closer to her. When he wasn't, she would become weak and want him to take care of her. When he did she would make

ACTIVITY #3
LISTENING WITH POSITIVE REGARD

1. Pick a topic to discuss. Choose one that is pleasurable for both of you.

2. One of you begin by making a brief statement about the topic. It doesn't have to be complete. Keep it to about 15 seconds.

3. Your partner should repeat back to you what he or she heard you say using the phrase, "I heard you say...." You listen; don't interrupt.

4. When your partner is finished, confirm that he or she heard you correctly by saying "Yes." If he or she didn't hear you correctly, repeat the part left out by saying, "I also said...." Or, if you felt your partner didn't hear you at all, repeat your statement again by saying, "I was trying to say...." Remember to keep it short.

5. It may be that your partner didn't hear your statement at all and can't repeat it. He or she may say, "I didn't hear what you said, would you please repeat it?" You then repeat exactly what you said. Don't add anything new or it will be confusing for your partner.

6. Once you're satisfied that your partner has heard you, it's your partner's turn to make a brief statement on the same topic.

7. You reflect your partner's statement back saying, "I heard you say...."

ACTIVITY #4
BLOWING YOUR COVER

Take turns telling each other your favorite ways to control each other by saying, "One of the ways I try to control you...." When you're doing this *listen* to your partner, but don't reply.

For example, you say, "One of the ways I try to control you is by being nice to you so you won't criticize me."

Your partner says, "One of the ways I try to control you, when I don't like what you're saying, is by yelling at you."

Do this four or five times. Then, using the technique of listening with positive regard, explore and discuss those favorite controls of yours so that each of you understands them well. You may also discover how you learned about those controls in your family.

herself available sexually. He decided to show her that he didn't really need her and could live quite happily without her. His career was a good vehicle for this because she couldn't condemn him for "just trying to keep ahead in a competitive world." He would also be above criticism from friends and family. This strategy only partially worked; although he would get sex occasionally, Allison was emotionally removed during it. After that kind of sex, he would feel more miserable than he did before. He would react by calling her cold and blaming her for his sexual dissatisfaction, which would lead to another round of arguments. But at least she didn't leave him.

If you want to move beyond the conflict and power struggles, you have to risk giving up some of your controls. One way to do this is by *blowing your cover*.

The purpose of this exercise is to clearly acknowledge to one another what is really happening when you become angry and frustrated with each other. It's a way of being open with each other, because the next time you try to control, your partner can say to you, "I think you're trying to control me right now. I have some criticisms of you; you're being nice and you know what a hard time I have when you're being so nice; I feel like it's all my fault and I shouldn't say anything." You can reply, "I think you're yelling at me now because you don't like to hear what I'm saying. This is important to me. I want to talk with you about it, but when you yell at me I feel attacked. I back off and think there's no use. I begin to give up on us."

If you can do this in a spirit of positive regard then you will be able to resolve your conflicts in a much more satisfying way. You will, however, have to take the risk of giving up your favorite controls, and being vulnerable. Don't worry though; you've got an endless supply! This alone will ensure that you will always have something interesting to talk about.

Blowing your cover can be a great source of fun and rib-tickling humor as you realize all the ridiculous ways you try to get your way. Some of them are absolutely infantile, many are downright devious, while others are totally ineffective. A good sense of humor can help you get through many conflicts with your self-respect intact.

6. It's my way or the highway

In the conflict/power struggle stage of relationship, people become firmly convinced that they are right about their view of what is wrong with the relationship. They take the stance of, "It's my way or the highway! *You* are the source of my unhappiness! I know what's wrong with *you!* It's your *fault!* I'm going to take *you* to the counselor so she can fix *you* up, then you'll give me what I want and I'll be happy." When you feel this way, ask yourself this question: "Would you rather keep on insisting that you're right than be happy?" People who have to be right all the time are the loneliest, most miserable people in the world. They are a drag to live with. Rightness destroys relationships.

EXAMPLE

Judy and Jim were well on their way toward developing an equal relationship. They had been able to work through many of their conflicts over the years. Jim had taken more responsibility for planning and cooking dinners. He fancied himself as a pretty good cook and, indeed, Judy appreciated his ability to serve good meals.

However, whenever Jim cooked he would only partially clean up the mess on the stove. This really bugged Judy. At first she asked Jim to clean up; when he didn't, she began to nag him. At parties when Jim would brag about his newly developed cooking skills Judy would manage to get in a dig at him that would embarrass and hurt him. They would fight about it on the way home. Jim chided her with "Why do you make such a fuss over such a small thing?"

This went on for about a year, until one evening it broke out into a full scale war. Judy lost her cool. She accused Jim of not caring about her. She told him she hated him for it. In seeing her rage for the first time over that issue, Jim realized that he had wanted his way in spite of Judy's requests for a change in his behavior. He did not value cleaning the stove immediately after cooking; next week was soon enough for him. Judy valued having a clean stove after each meal. It gave her a sense of completion.

Before the confrontation, Jim had maintained that, on this issue, he would rather be right than happy. He stubbornly insisted that his way was more important than his love for Judy. After the confrontation he understood that one of the ways he could express his love for Judy would be to clean the stove after each meal, even though it was something that he did not particularly value. It would be, from Judy's perspective, a profound expression of caring. He changed his position to wanting to be happy with Judy rather than stubbornly insisting on having it his own way.

Being willing and able to recognize when you have adopted the stance of "It's my way or the highway" is the first step to getting to the heart of your power struggles. To ask, in the heat of battle, "Is it more important to get my own way than to clear up this disagreement?" is to examine your intentions. "Am I looking for a way to build our love and trust?" These are the questions that let you be clear about your intentions and open to seeing the other's point of view.

The issue of surrender is wrapped up with rightness. If your relationship is ever going to work in terms of supporting each other's well-being, you must be willing to surrender to each other. If you look up the word "surrender" in *Webster's Dictionary*, you will find that the first definition is "to give up possession of or power over." To assert that you would rather be right at any cost is an attempt to maintain your power over the other person and never let that person have influence over you. Willingness to surrender is an expression of deep and profound love.

Happy people know what's right for them. They live by their own standards. They also acknowledge that others have values, opinions, and ways of doing things that are different from their own but still valid. Joy, laughter, mutual respect, and a shared inner peace are the payoffs for a couple who choose happiness over rightness. They are earned by those who have the skills and courage to negotiate the inevitable conflicts and power struggles that occur in relationships.

d. THE RESIGNATION OR REALITY STAGE

1. Resignation

If you don't resolve your power struggles but stay in the relationship, you will resign yourself to the relationship in its state of conflict. This will come about after yet another round of fights and hassles or cold, silent battles.

The signs of resignation may be familiar: you just can't keep on living like this; both of you sense the weariness; an unspoken truce is called; a period of anxious peace pervades the atmosphere; you are careful not to step on each other's toes. Your conflicts have not been resolved but a stability is established. You become cautiously friendly. Sex, if there's any at all, becomes as perfunctory as taking out the garbage on Friday. Each of you goes about your daily activities with businesslike smoothness. You might occasionally enjoy a momentary romantic interlude when a spark of hope is re-ignited in your hearts that will cause you to wistfully lament the passing of your more carefree days together.

You can adjust to each other for a limited time only. Before you know it, another angry flare-up pushes you back into the unresolved conflicts. You fight over the same things. Your arguments are boringly repetitive. At parties friends roll their eyes and say, "There go Sam and Diane again — at each other's throats."

Some couples, tired of the cyclical hassles, make a pact never to discuss anything important as a way of avoiding the conflicts. While co-habitating they assume a life of independence, each finding excitement in career, children, friendships, hobbies, or politics. Their agreed-upon distance allows them to live a comfortable, efficient life together. Many of our parents made this choice.

One of the main characteristics of resignation is that each partner complains to people outside the relationship. Any attempt to help or mediate by friends, family, or counselors is rebuffed. The clear intention is to maintain the status quo. Usually it requires a crisis of major proportions before a couple is hurled out of their resigned, boring relationship. Typical crises are affairs, serious illnesses, children leaving home, unemployment, financial disasters, death or birth of children, or moves from one city to another.

2. Reality

To confront your conflicts and power struggles is to choose to deal with reality.

Each time you resolve a conflict your individuality blossoms. You become a more interesting person to your partner. To choose reality is to allow yourself to see the good, the bad, the ugly, and the beautiful sides of your partner. Out of this comes a feeling of safety based on knowing who your partner is. You are with a real person, not a straw man or frail waif.

Reality has its risks. Within each of us there is a fear of revealing too much. This fear is based on the assumption that if your partner really gets to know you he or she will not like you. However, if you take the risk and are accepted you will know that you are loved just because you're you and you can stop running around trying to prove you're lovable. Your partner was swept off his or her feet at the romantic stage for very particular reasons, most of which he or she was not aware of. At this stage those attractions will become reality. Your partner will be even more fascinated with you, if you are both willing to risk being open and appreciating each other's complexity.

Let's return to Jim and Allison's story. Part of Jim's reality is that he is afraid of being close to Allison or anyone else. By his criticism he pushes her away and feels more comfortable, but lonely. He attempts to fill the lonely void by overworking. Reality for Allison is accepting that she is a very strong person — stronger than she is willing to admit. By confronting Jim she regains the sense of self-esteem that she lost in her overly critical family.

One of the ugly facts that Jim must face about himself is that he is a coward when confronted by a strong woman. He's afraid to ask directly for what he wants. He hides behind his mask of independence, while at the same time feeling victimized by Allison. One of Allison's uglies is that she picked Jim as her mouthpiece to the world. She is afraid to say what she really thinks.

She hides her judgments because she wants everyone to accept her.

With these realities out in the open, Jim and Allison make a choice to engage in an equal relationship. They can now help each other build on their strengths and overcome their weaknesses.

If you do show yourself in all your glory and you are rejected, at least you will know why. Besides, your partner is probably not rejecting the real you. He or she is either unwilling or unable to forgive you for what went on during the conflict/power struggle stage or refuses to let go of his or her out-dated image of you. You will recognize that it is your partner's problem, not yours. You will emerge from the relationship perhaps sad, but with your self-esteem intact.

EXAMPLE

Sara and Bill got together as the result of a mutual dream of running their own business so that they could be their own bosses. They worked hard over the years and were materially successful. Sara was ready to let go of the responsibilities and enjoy her success. Bill continued to work as hard as the day they opened the business. They had entered counseling because they no longer had any enjoyable sex life. In counseling it became clear that Bill was not about to let down; he was too afraid. Sara was confronted with the realization that Bill was not going to change. If she wanted to realize her dreams it was going to be without Bill. She left him and he bought her out. She began to travel and had the time of her life. Six years later Bill was confined to a wheelchair following a stroke.

During the reality stage, you must make clear what you want in your relationship. Few of us can ask for what we want in a joyful, open fashion without guilt. As children we were told that it was rude to ask and that it was more polite to wait to be invited. There are millions of people still waiting to be asked. If you never ask, you'll probably never get what you want. Your life will consist of what's left over after you've avoided all the things you are afraid of. Since all of us are afraid of almost everything, that leaves practically nothing.

If you think it's rude to ask but you feel compelled to ask, you will likely ask for things apologetically. If you think it's rude to ask but believe that you deserve what you're asking for, you'll probably grab angrily for it, thereby alienating the person. One of the keys to joy and equality in relationship is to develop the ability to ask for what you want in a way that allows your partner to either refuse graciously or feel delighted to give it to you.

You must learn how to make demands. Demands at this reality stage are based on what is missing in your relationship. They originate in the desire to make the relationship authentic. By resolving your conflicts and power struggles you've recognized that your partner is a person with weaknesses as well as strengths. You have experienced your own individuality. You appreciate that a loving relationship means intense interaction — both positive and negative. The issue is engagement. To engage your partner means to make demands, to confront, to be open to saying yes without reservations, and to risk saying no with conviction, not anger. Mutual respect, gained through the satisfactory resolution of your conflicts and power struggles, is a necessity. Equality is the by-product.

Love at the reality stage is not for the fainthearted! To make demands and to respect your partner's demands is difficult. It means you possess a sense of entitlement. You accurately know and feel what is your due. Patience, perspective, and staying

power are required. You must also be willing to risk failure: better no relationship at all than one that does not work or one in which love does not grow. The guiding principle is this: Only when you make clear demands can your partner cope, respond, and adapt to them. Demands not made cannot be integrated into the living relationship. Most engagement, of course, should be positive. The result is a strong love bond and an enduring connection.

Of course, if you are going to make demands, you must know what you want in a relationship. People generally want an experience of themselves as lovable and capable people. Assume that your partner wants the same. None of your demands should be used to control or use your partner in a way that would lower her or his self-esteem.

To develop your skills for making demands try the following activity. When you and your partner have worked through the exercise and have made your demands known to each other, you are ready for the next stage.

e. THE FULL COMMITMENT STAGE

A truly loving relationship requires commitment. Clinical philosopher Dr. Peter Koestenbaum calls it "the decision to care." All relationships go through trying times — economic or psychological crises, illnesses, deep disappointments, or betrayals. In each case, expressing your love may mean self-sacrificing devotion and loyal, unrequited caring during an acute period. That is the nature of ethical love; it is the result of a promise made and kept.

When couples make a commitment at the romantic stage, it is not usually based on rational considerations. This is particularly evident if you examine the divorce statistics, observe an unhappy marriage, or listen to the dissatisfaction voiced about male/female relationships. Marriage today is equivalent to booking passage on the Titanic knowing full well that the thing is going to sink but not knowing whether you'll be one of the survivors.

In our view, the process of getting married itself is a woman's ritual. The man is almost completely ignored and excluded from the wedding plans. He may be consulted, but for all intents and purposes the wedding ritual is the fulfillment of the woman's fantasy, not the man's. The problem is not the existence of the fantasy, but that the man is not committed to the elaborate preparations. Thus from the very beginning of the relationship he is only partially committed. He bears some of the responsibility for this situation by going along with it rather than fighting for a place in it. The woman contributes to the probable failure of the relationship by not making sure that the man is 100% committed to the process.

The average wedding costs about $10,200. Most couples do not spend one cent on any kind of marriage preparation program that would help them examine the depth of their commitment. Thus their commitments are usually based on hollow promises and unrealistic dreams.

1. The decision to care

The decision to care at the commitment stage is a rational obligation. It is based on your mutual history made meaningful through your accumulated triumphs and tribulations of the previous four stages. We've asked couples who have been married for 20 to 30 years why they thought their marriages had lasted. They usually say that it was their partner's willingness to stand by them and love them during the difficult times that helped them endure.

EXAMPLE

At 11:45 p.m., Thursday, April 14, 1985 Julie told Michael about her year-long affair with a colleague. He remembers the details vividly because his whole world had just crumbled before him. He had no idea this was going on. He thought their relationship was a good one. He had not realized how unhappy Julie had been. His entire body pulsed and groaned as if it was about to explode. His mind went blank, then his entire being slipped into a painful numbness. After the initial shock, his immediate gut reaction was to beat her up and throw her out into the

ACTIVITY #5
ASKING FOR WHAT YOU WANT

On the top of three separate sheets of paper write the following:

1. What I want more of from my partner in this relationship is....
2. What I want less of from my partner is....
3. What's just right in this relationship is....

Complete those phrases as many times as you are able. Ask your partner to do the same. Give yourselves two to three hours over a couple of days to complete the activity. The more thought you put into it the more you will gain from the exercise.

Set aside some uninterrupted time to have a conversation about what you've written. Remember to listen with positive regard.

street where all tramps belong. He didn't. He realized that he still cared for her. At this moment he couldn't say he loved her. In spite of his deep hurt he decided to stand by Julie, if she wanted him to, to work out their difficulties. Julie agreed but made it clear that she had a lot of unresolved conflicts with him; for now, she was committed to resolving their problems but she was not committed to their relationship. With those commitments Julie and Michael began counseling to clear up their unresolved conflicts and power struggles.

There are two lessons to be learned in the above example. The first is that one person can be at one stage while the other is at another. Julie was at the conflict/power struggle stage, but was unwilling to confront that truth. Michael was happily at the commitment stage unwilling or unable to see Julie's deep dissatisfaction.

The second lesson is that relationships are sloppy. They don't fit neatly into some theoretical package. Reading a book will not solve your problems although it may point the way to taking the steps that are required. Relationships must be lived out, not read about.

2. Being yourself in relationship

To make a commitment is to believe in romanticism. Romantic love is a beautiful experience; it opens your heart and stirs your romantic passions. It adds a sparkle of color and radiance to an otherwise pedestrian world. However, you can't build a satisfying life by falling in love every day, or by expecting romance to last. The solution is to develop your capacity to periodically recapture and renew your romantic perception. It happens when you and your partner make a commitment to each other. You know that your partner cares in spite of having seen the good, the bad, the ugly, and the beautiful. As a result, you can create a mature romanticism that combines the imagination of the romantic stage with the realism of the reality stage.

Through commitment you can create a true partnership expressed in the statement, "I want to be with you." It's what we call being yourself in relationship. It means that you are going to work out with each other the essentially conflicting goals of freedom and intimacy, of separateness and unity, of aloneness and sharing. In doing so you make a commitment to keep your relationship loving, fresh, alive, interesting, and authentic.

Commitment demands purpose or meaning that can be made concrete. "Work is love made visible," wrote Gibran. The task in the next stage is to make your love visible.

f. THE MATURE ROMANCE STAGE

The challenge of this stage is to gaze, not at each other, but outward in the same direction. You stand together facing the world. You make yourselves part of the community of humankind through your career, by raising your children, in religion, in recreation, with community service, or in education, but between you is a bond of truly equal partnership that you have lovingly forged in the previous stages. The love you feel can only be described as romantic, but it is a romance that has matured and been tempered by your developing intimacy. Your excitement and creativity emerges from the fact that you are two unique individuals deciding to be in a relationship.

The skills that you acquired in the previous stages will be tested in this stage as you struggle to attain your place in the world, remain open to love, and keep in touch with your inner self. This stage is as difficult as any of the others.

1. Values and priorities

Your values and priorities provide a reference point to which you can turn as you are buffeted by life's struggles, disappointments, and temptations. The world is full of opportunities and attractive sideshows with which you can become mesmerized: promotions, transfers, power, material pursuits, handsome bodies, sharp minds, the latest fads. You name it, the carnival of life offers it. By knowing your values and priorities you can choose what is important to you and you can control the direction and intensity of your life. The following activity will be helpful in clarifying your most important values.

Establishing your priorities is an exercise in making your commitments visible. Living according to your values makes the commitments tangible. Take turns with your partner describing your values and priorities to each other. Remember to listen with positive regard.

Your individual lists will help you clarify and decide what your chosen lifestyle will be. The similarities in your values are the origins of your compatibility. If your values are very similar you will have a degree of compatibility that may verge on boredom, so you will have to find ways to create excitement. The differences in your values provide a source of excitement in your relationship. Differences that you don't accept are the source of your conflicts. If you have many differences in values your relationship will be exciting and full of conflict. You will spend a lot of time working out your conflicts and power struggles. In either case, you will have to negotiate ways to help each other live according to your values.

2. Contract for intimacy

The need to clarify your values and priorities at this stage is based on the assumption that you are willing to do whatever you can to help your partner fulfill his or her potential and vice versa. For this to happen, you need a mutually agreed upon "contract" that defines the framework of your relationship. The contract answers the question, "How can we encourage each other to develop our individuality while being in a relationship?" Your contract should set out specific behaviors that are desired as well as those that will not be tolerated by each of you.

In such a relationship there is mutual dependency that evolves, not out of helplessness, but out of choice and out of the recognition of your own values as well as your partner's. You agree to depend on each other so that each of you can live according to your individual values. It's a dependency that develops out of the awareness of each of your personal resources that you bring to the relationship.

In negotiating the contract you also spell out and agree to accept the other's independence. There is a dynamic flow between dependence and independence so that either of you can assume the leadership role to fit a specific situation. When there is conflict, you can resolve it within the context of the values that each person maintains for himself or herself.

One of the signs that you have reached the mature romance stage is that you have the energy to do creative things that extend beyond yourself and that have an effect on other relationships around you. Another is that your relationship becomes a refuge from the world, a place where you can relax and rejuvenate. A little time at home together boosts your energy.

g. CONCLUSION

The journey through the six stages of relationship is haphazard and sloppy. You don't progress neatly from one to the other. But with persistence and patience two people can create a loving relationship that endures. When you have cycled through

ACTIVITY #6
HOW TO TELL WHETHER YOU ARE AT THE CONFLICT/POWER STRUGGLE STAGE OR THE COMMITMENT STAGE

Check off statements in each column that apply to your situation.

☐ Knowledge of the other is used as a weapon for control.

☐ A sense of safety is absent. I feel that I have to protect myself from my partner.

☐ Authority and control are rigidly maintained or pursued as a means of gaining power over the other. Our arguments are polarized into who is right and who is wrong.

☐ One of us feels dominant, the other feels dominated. The "dominant" partner assumes more worth by virtue of having power and control over the other partner.

☐ Loyalty is demanded as an instrument of control and power. It often seems to be a matter of choosing sides.

☐ Communication is guarded, wary, and is often used to gain information for more power and control over the other.

☐ One or both of us is often trying to get something from the other. The other often seems to be withholding it.

☐ Our fights often turn into a struggle over who can get most control, have more power, and win. Love, affection, and intimacy seem far off.

☐ As we get to know each other more our intimacy is deepened.

☐ Each of us feels safe enough to be ourselves when we are together. We respect each other's point of view.

☐ Authority and control alternates between the two of us, depending on the needs and capabilities of each of us in a particular situation. We have little trouble, most of the time, giving up or taking control.

☐ Each of us sees the other as being worthy of being loved just because he or she is alive. We don't have to prove our love for each other.

☐ We put each other as number one priority in our personal life.

☐ Our communications are open, clear, candid, and most often result in more intimacy.

☐ We see each other as unique individuals, and we respect that individuality.

☐ We have few doubts about whether we want to be together. We take responsibility for the fact that we choose to be in this relationship exclusively.

If you checked off at least 4 of the statements in the lefthand column, you are in the conflict/power struggle stage. A score of 6 to 8 indicates you are locked in a serious power struggle.

If you checked off 4 or more of the statements in the righthand column you are into the commitment stage. Of course, the more you checked off the more you are committed.

Read over the values that are described below. The definitions given are suggestions. Substitute your own definitions if you wish. In the three blank spaces, write in any values that you want to add. Number, in order of priority, 10 values that are important to you. Your partner should complete this exercise too.

_____ Loyalty: Maintaining important connections and commitments

_____ Power: Having authority and influence

_____ Independence: Having freedom of thought and action

_____ Education: Continuing growth in knowledge and skills

_____ Recognition: Receiving recognition for achievements

_____ Emotional well-being: solving emotional problems and having self-esteem

_____ Spiritual well-being: Living according to my spiritual beliefs

_____ Physical well-being: Taking care of my body

_____ Sexual fulfillment: Feeling good about myself sexually

_____ Quality marriage/relationship: Having a marriage/relationship that is a source of love and fulfillment

_____ Love: Loving and be loved

_____ Success and achievement: Being able to do things really well

_____ Pleasure/joy: Enjoying the joy and pleasures in my life

_____ Family: Maintaining family traditions and background

_____ Parenthood: Having and taking care of children as a source of fulfillment

_____ Aesthetics: Having beauty in my surroundings

_____ Acceptance: Being accepted by people who are important to me

_____ Uniqueness: Being my own, unique creative self

_____ Sports and hobbies: Having recreational activities I enjoy

_____ Openness: Being open and truthful with the people I love

_____ Career/work: Having a job/career/vocation that is fulfilling

_____ Financial security: Being secure today, building financial resources for the future

_____ Integrity: Living by ethical standards

_____ Prestige: Having status in my community

_____ _____

_____ _____

_____ _____

When you have both completed this task, talk together using the instructions outlined on page 25 in the section " Learning how to listen with positive regard."

all the stages once, don't expect your relationship to remain within the neat package of "...and they lived happily ever after." You will return to the other stages as you confront different issues. To make it even more interesting there will be times when each of you are at different stages. Each time you cycle through the stages your skills, competency, and love will grow as you create your "experienced history" together.

A relationship is like a garden. It requires tending. Unhealthy things need to be weeded out. Some plants have to be nurtured, cultivated, and watched carefully as they grow. Each season demands different activities. Daily weeding, clipping, and watering keeps the garden fresh, fertile, and alive. Neglect it for a year or two and you face months of back-breaking restoration work. Some plants may never recover. Leave it for too long and you'll have to start all over again from scratch.

A well-tended garden has a healing energy that is obvious to any who visit it. It has warmth and color, and it brings joy to the hearts of those who carefully, lovingly, and (sometimes) painfully nurture it.

Like a garden, developing a loving, fulfilling relationship requires time, intention, and knowledge. It cannot be hurried. It is created in space and in time out of the substance of life itself.

4

ASSESSING YOUR RELATIONSHIP

In this chapter you have an opportunity to diagnose the current health of your relationship, discover how self-disclosure can get you on the path to intimacy, make an assessment of your basic relationship skills, and learn how to give and receive feedback so that you can begin to identify and deal with the sources of your problems and conflicts.

You need more than impulse, intuition, blind luck, or even common sense to create a satisfying, loving relationship. Yet many people become anxious, mystified, or defensive when they realize they need to do something about their relationship. Some individuals find the issue too threatening to deal with directly, so they do nothing, hoping the problems will go away. Others try to cope with their difficulties by taking a vacation together, "without the kids and away from the phone." Some couples think that going out for a candlelight dinner or learning a new hobby together will solve their problems. Those efforts are usually in vain; loving relationships rarely succeed or fail on superficialities.

You can learn to understand what you want and need from your partner, and your partner can do the same. But to do this you have to know the current state of your relationship. You can learn to strengthen what is working well and develop your skills for improving the weaknesses. Often your attitudes toward your partner will be the major stumbling block to creating intimacy. If you can develop an awareness of those attitudes, you will be better able to control and overcome them.

Building an environment in which you feel close to each other and able to deal with the inevitable conflicts and problems that arise in any relationship requires time and effort. You may have to stretch yourself in new and unfamiliar ways, but it is well worth the effort. A loving, satisfying relationship is one of the keys to a healthy, happy life.

a. THE RELATIONSHIP CHECKLIST

The place to begin developing your relationship is to take a look at its current status. The relationship checklist on the next page will help you do just that.

1. What your score means

If your score is between 11 and 22, from your point of view you and your partner are handling day-to-day issues well. If your partner's score is in this range, then both of you are probably feeling okay about your relationship. Keep up the good work. However, if your partner has a higher score than you, each of you has a different perspective on the current state of health of the relationship. You need to talk about those differences, as they are potential sources of frustration, conflict, or anger.

If your score is between 23 and 33, there is some evidence that various aspects of your relationship are in need of attention. You need to identify exactly what is troubling you so that you and your partner can

ACTIVITY #8
RELATIONSHIP CHECKLIST

The checklist below is designed to give you some idea about the general state of health of your relationship. You and your partner should complete the checklist separately, then read the sections on scoring and guidlines for discussion before talking together about your individual assessments. Circle the number on the scale of 1 to 5 that applies to your relationship *as you see it*.

	Never				Very often
1. Feeling of low energy or lack of enthusiasm about the relationship	1	2	3	4	5
2. Unresolved conflict between you and your partner	1	2	3	4	5
3. Apathy or general lack of interest or involvement between you and your partner	1	2	3	4	5
4. Lack of clear resolution about problems or disagreements; discussions "go in circles"	1	2	3	4	5
5. Poor communication - fear of speaking up, not listening to each other, or not talking to each other	1	2	3	4	5
6. Dissatisfaction about how much your partner contributes to the relationship or shares in work around the home	1	2	3	4	5
7. Not much interest in or not much satisfaction with sex in the relationship	1	2	3	4	5
8. Feelings of being trapped and that you can't be yourself with your partner	1	2	3	4	5
9. Feeling of being put down by your partner when with friends	1	2	3	4	5
10. Feelings of greater ease when your partner is not around	1	2	3	4	5
11. Many thoughts about "splitting" from your partner	1	2	3	4	5

Now add up your total score for the 11 items.

deal with those areas before they become a major source of conflict. *If your or your partner rated two or three items in the high evidence range, these particular issues are major trouble spots.* They must be dealt with immediately or they will negate the good things you have going for you. By completing the activities and carefully reading the rest of the book with your partner, you will likely be able to clear up your difficulties.

If your score is between 34 and 43, you already know your relationship is not satisfying for you. You and your partner must have a serious discussion about your dissatisfactions. Go through each item in the checklist and talk specifically about how you arrived at your scores. Follow the guidelines outlined in the next section, or your discussion is likely to turn into a fight. If you find yourselves getting bogged down in a verbal battle, keep reading this book and make arrangements today to see a counselor. If you let things slide, you will likely be in crisis soon. See chapter 9 for tips on how to choose a relationship counselor.

If you score is over 43, your relationship is in trouble. While this book can help you understand the dynamics of relationships, you are in need of outside help. If your partner's score is 34 or more, you are looking at long-term counseling. But don't despair. If *both* of you recognize the need for help and are willing to put time and effort into working on your problems, you can revive your relationship, however hopeless it may look.

We do not subscribe to the idea that two people are "just not made for each other." We ourselves went though our own difficulties in our relationship and split up for a year. When we decided to get counseling, one of our friends said to us, "If you two can make it through this, anybody can." We did, but it was hard work. It took a couple of years of intensive, expensive counseling, plus a lot of effort on our part.

We now feel we have a truly loving, intimate relationship.

We are not implying that you *should* stay together under any circumstances. Sometimes it's best to acknowledge that the relationship isn't working and move on. If your partner is unwilling to go to a counselor, it is still advantageous for you to do so on your own so that you can talk to an objective person and gain some peace of mind. See chapter 9 on how to choose a relationship counselor.

2. Guidelines for effective discussion

Before you talk with your partner about your scores, read the following guidelines.

(a) Concentrate on listening to what is being said. Talk one at a time. If you don't agree with what your partner is saying, concentrate on listening and understanding. It's important that you really hear what the other is saying. If you are in a long-term relationship, you probably know one another quite well in certain ways; for example, you are able to predict what your partner will do or say in certain situations. The difficulty is that you probably don't understand the underlying reasons for the behavior, although you may think you do. By listening carefully, you'll begin to understand your partner more.

EXAMPLE

Jean and Ray have just finished their checklist and are discussing their findings.

Jean: I have some unresolved conflict with you, Ray, so I circled 4 on that item. It's about how I think you leave most of the housework to me.

Ray: I was afraid of this. You have some unresolved conflict with me around my sharing the housework.

Jean: Yes, I want you to take more responsibility for the household chores, such as cleaning and vacuuming.

Ray: You want me to take more responsibility for the household chores like cleaning and vacuuming.

Jean: Okay, let's leave it at that for now until we read more of the book.

(b) Remember that what you're hearing is your partner's perspective. Each of you is entitled to your own thoughts, feelings, and opinions. One of the reasons many couples get into so much difficulty is that they are not willing to listen to each other's point of view. This is why arguments go around in circles. In order to resolve differences, you must be willing to acknowledge that they exist. If you think everything is just fine in your relationship while your partner tells you that he or she is unhappy, you've got a problem. Your partner's unhappiness is going to affect your relationship. The best thing you can do is listen carefully to the source of that unhappiness and together find ways of resolving the problem.

(c) If you don't understand your partner, use the following statement to gain clarification: "I don't understand. Would you please explain it to me." The reason for using this statement is that many couples, when they don't understand each other, will say, "You don't make sense," or, "You're wrong." These kind of inflammatory statements usually elicit a defensive, angry reaction, and the conversation degenerates into a useless argument. When you say, "I don't understand," you are taking responsibility for that fact. When you say, "Would you please explain it to me," you are showing common courtesy for your partner (which must be genuine, of course) that he

or she will appreciate. These little things can keep the lines of communication open in times of conflict.

Now that you have some idea of the state of health of your relationship, the next step is to decide whether you want to do something about it. If you and your partner do want to start redeveloping your love, trust, and intimacy, a good place to begin is by going back to where you started when you first met — by being more open with each other and disclosing yourself to your partner.

In chapter 7 you will learn how to deal with conflict and anger. For now, concentrate on diagnosing and understanding the current state of your problems, not solving them. If you try to find solutions now without the skill development, you'll just get frustrated.

Before proceeding, we'd like to tell you one of our favorite stories. To us, unhappy or troubled relationships are like those huge balls of string that accumulate in a junk drawer. Usually you're in a hurry when you want a piece of string, and you swear a bit as you try to pull out a piece long enough to use. It never works of course — the more you pull, the tighter the whole ball becomes. The only way to get a length of string long enough is to patiently untangle the seemingly infinite number of knots, so that slowly but surely a usable piece of string emerges and you can get the job done.

The same is true of troubled relationships. You have to patiently unravel the knots that have grown over the years. There is, of course, a major difference between a ball of string and your relationship. You can't do it alone — it takes two to untangle the knots.

b. SELF-DISCLOSURE

Self-disclosure is the process by which you directly and consciously let another person know the thoughts and feelings that are going on inside you. It includes telling about significant events in your life history, especially those events that are still affecting your behavior today. Decisions about whether to disclose yourself are a constant part of everyday life. Should you reveal your thoughts, feelings, or past to another person? How intimate should your disclosures be? What are the appropriate places and times to talk about yourself? Whom should you tell?

The decisions you make about self-disclosure will have a major impact on your life. Those decisions can influence the number of friends you have and how well they know you. Your level of self-disclosure will determine the extent of your happiness and satisfaction in life. Your decisions about the amount, the type, and the timing of your self-disclosure will affect the depth of your self-awareness as well as your sense of individuality (personalities #1 and #2 in chapter 2).

Self-disclosure is necessary to establish and maintain loving, long-term relationships. An intimate relationship is one in which the highest level of self-disclosure is expected and accepted. An intimate partner serves as a confidant and best friend — someone with whom you can explore fears and joys. The willingness to share intimacies attests to the closeness of a couple. A willingness to divulge personal, sometimes embarrassing material demonstrates the sense of safety each feels in the relationship.

One rule of thumb we have found helpful in our relationship is that any persistent thought or feeling needs to be expressed, no matter how small it may seem, how embarrassing it is to say, or how scared of saying it we may be. Holding it back only serves to create a sense of alienation and misunderstanding between us. Over time the withholding can contaminate every area of our relationship, so that small dis-

agreements quickly escalate into major wars.

EXAMPLES

1. Jack and Susan have been seeing each other for about a year. In the last four months Jack feels that Susan has been withdrawing from him. He thinks that she is not interested in him any more. One night he tells her about his feelings, Susan breaks into tears, then tells Jack about the problems she has been having with her alcoholic father. She hasn't wanted to tell him about it because she was afraid Jack would reject her. He tells her he still loves her. Their relationship moves to a new and deeper level.

2. Tracy is thinking about leaving Robert. She now realizes that she has never really known him. For six years, she has lived with him, cooked and cleaned for him, and slept with him. In all that time, they have talked only about day-to-day things, such as what was planned for dinner, their vacation plans, or what car to buy next. Robert has never talked with Tracy about his hopes, his dreams, or his feelings, even though she has asked him to on many occasions. She feels terribly lonely with him and now wants to move on with her life. Better to be in no relationship at all than to be in one in which she feels so lonely.

3. Sharon and Ken have been married for eight years. They have two children and a nice home. Ken is a good father and provider. Sharon has her own business which she runs out of the house. To their friends, Sharon and Ken have the perfect relationship. Yesterday Ken confessed to a six-month long affair

with one of their mutual friends. Sharon is shocked; she thought they had a good marriage. Ken has never complained about anything. Yesterday Ken said he hasn't been happy about their sex life for a few years now, but didn't want to tell her for fear of hurting her feelings. This crisis could have been avoided had Ken disclosed himself much sooner.

4. Steve and Julie were married three years ago. Julie had lived on her own for five years before meeting Steve. They are both managers in their respective companies. After they got married, Steve took over the management of the finances, including Julie's paycheck. Julie now feels she has to beg for her spending money and resents Steve for that. Eighteen months ago they had a baby. Julie has been back at her job for three months now. She feels she takes 95% of the responsibility for looking after their son, buying the groceries, and taking care of the house. Last week she went to see the company nurse because she didn't understand why she felt so uptight and angry at her co-workers, her child, and her husband. In that meeting it became clear to her that she was trying to be a superwoman and needed to get a lot of things off her chest. After the meeting she felt a lot better. Her next task is to clear up her accumulated resentments toward her husband.

Many people in relationships feel lonely and isolated, even though they live under the same roof with another person. One or both of the partners can feel this sense of alienation. When you feel alienated, you usually also feel isolated from almost everything that makes life meaningful — work, friends, and self. You feel powerless to influence the course of your own life. Depressed, confused, and uncertain, you withdraw further and further from your partner and perhaps from your friends. In its extreme forms, alienation can lead to a so-called nervous breakdown, spending sprees, affairs, or suicide. But the sense of isolation is a signal from your unconscious to do something about your present state of affairs. It is trying to give you the message to come out of yourself and say what's on your mind. Your unconscious is your best and wisest friend. It wants you to be happy. Listen to it!

EXAMPLE

Jim: "I remember going to bed one night after a silent evening with Judy in which the air was filled with many unsaid things. Judy crawled into one side of the bed, I into the other. She faced one wall, I faced the other. We didn't even so much as say goodnight to each other. In the other room, our lovely daughter lay sleeping innocently in her crib. At that moment I felt a deep pain in my chest as I thought about us. Here we were, two good people, who had chosen to be together because we loved each other. Now we were 100 miles apart in our silence. I felt totally isolated and alone, even though Judy lay not six inches away from me. I didn't sleep at all that night. The next morning I told Judy about my feelings. We began to talk about the things we were holding back. It was painful, but we haven't looked back since, nor have I felt that kind of loneliness with her again."

One positive result of self-disclosure is that it promotes self-awareness. If you hide yourself from others, they cannot respond to your problems or your good feelings, nor can they help you understand your unrevealed feelings or thoughts. You may hide your innermost self because you fear that you are the only one who thinks or feels those kinds of things. But this sets up a catch-22 situation. Just as others do not know the person who reveals little, so he or she does not know others. People are unlikely to reveal themselves wholeheartedly to you if you do not disclose yourself in return. It's a two-way street.

If you are a person who discloses little, you will be unable to perceive and understand the complex motivations and emotions that characterize human beings because your experience with others will be limited to superficial contact. In fact, we find that those who disclose little about themselves will demand that their partners "stop talking about themselves so much" or "stop the navel-gazing." But by complying, the partner will become cut off, alienated from his or her own being as well as others.

Alternatively, when you disclose yourself the people around you will respond in one way or another, and it is in that interchange of responses that you will get to know more of yourself and others. Some of your newfound knowledge may be difficult to swallow, but better to walk around in the bright sun of awareness than to grope in the dense fog of ignorance.

EXAMPLE

George: "One night Alice and I were beginning to make love according to our usual routine. After 15 years we had it down pat. I had been really bored with our lovemaking for about 10 years, but I continued on thinking that it pleased her. Anyway, this particular night I said, 'Alice, I'm really bored with what we do in bed. I don't enjoy it anymore and I find myself wishing it were over almost as soon as we start.'"

Alice: "I was shocked, angry, and afraid. But then I broke out laughing, because I had been thinking the same thing for a long time but hadn't said anything for fear of hurting George's feelings. We talked long into the morning about our ideas about sex and how we had been raised to treat sex as bad. We even talked about the disaster of our wedding night. It was the best thing that ever happened to our relationship."

Many couples report that they don't disclose themselves to each other because they don't trust their partners. Most books on marriage say that you must trust each other before you can begin to disclose yourself. We disagree. Our view is that trust comes about *after* you disclose yourself. But more importantly, to disclose yourself in the face of your fear of doing so means that you will experience your courage. When you experience your courage you become a healthier human being because you develop trust in your own inner strength. This knowledge will get you through anything with your self-esteem intact.

But what if you disclose yourself and your partner punishes you, makes fun of you, or uses the information against you in the future? We think that is a risk worth taking. Our view is that it is better to know what kind of person you are living with so that you can make a very clear decision about whether or not you want to be with him or her. If you disclose yourself and, say, your partner makes fun of you or tells you're crazy, your partner has shown you his or her attitudes toward you. That is a painful truth, but in the long run it is helpful to have that knowledge. You now know what kind of person you are dealing with. You can then make the decision either to stay and confront your partner or to leave what may be an untenable situation. Conversely, if you disclose something embarrassing about yourself and your partner treats you with respect, empathy, and reciprocal openness, you know that your partner is a person with whom you can enjoy being yourself.

Personal, intimate love of another person requires that you really know the other. That's why love deepens over time as you reveal more of yourselves to each other. Conversely, if you withhold yourself from your partner, it will be impossible for him or her to love you in any personal way. Your partner might be able to love you as a human being, but he or she won't have that special love for you that is created in mutually intimate relationships. Moreover, in your secretiveness you will be incapable of loving your partner, because when you withhold yourself you also shut the door on truly knowing your partner.

The following activity is designed to help you both discover more about yourselves and then disclose your findings to each other.

c. GIVING AND RECEIVING FEEDBACK

When you disclose yourself, you open the door to creating an intimate relationship. By giving, asking for, and receiving feedback, you invite another into your private world to hear what the other thinks about you. It's a risky thing to do, because the perception you have of your self and your world can be very different from even your closest friend's perception. Giving, asking for, and receiving feedback implies that you are open to another's point of view even though it may be different from yours. It may result in your whole world being turned upside down, or confirmed.

EXAMPLES

1. Sandy was having an argument with Beryl. It erupted into a shouting match and ended by the two of them stomping off in a huff. Kerrie, Sandy's lifetime confidant, witnessed the entire exchanged.

Sandy: Beryl is such a stubborn pig-headed fool. She won't listen to anything you say. Wouldn't you agree?

Kerrie: Are you sure you're willing to hear what I have to say, because I saw it differently?

Sandy: (Shaking in his boots) Yes.

Kerrie: Actually, in my opinion you were acting bull-headed and arrogant. To me, you weren't listening to Beryl at all. I thought you shouted her down as soon as she began to disagree with you. It seemed to me that she couldn't get a word in edgewise.

Sandy asked for the feedback and now it is his responsibility to consider what Kerrie has said to him. He can reject it, accept it, or modify it to fit in with his innermost experience. Probably the most effective thing he could do would be to talk with Beryl again, tell Beryl what Kerrie said, and attempt to overcome the misunderstanding. In any event, he will have learned something about himself.

2. Nancy took up painting a few years ago and has become quite accomplished, to the extent of having a local gallery ask her to exhibit a couple of her works. Ron walked into her studio with a cup of tea for her.

Ron: My, that's very good. I like the way you've blended the colors and highlighted the contrasts.

Nancy: I don't like the way it's turned out. I think I'm losing my touch. Maybe I'll throw it away.

Ron: Oh, I guess you don't want to hear what I have to say. Is that so?

ACTIVITY #9
RELATIONSHIP SKILLS: A SELF-CHECK

Step 1

Listed below are the 10 basic skills that are needed to establish a satisfying, loving relationship. Read over each of them carefully before you rate yourself. Make sure you understand each one.

Step 2

Working on your own, rate your level of skill development. Go through the list and circle one of the numbers under each skill described, *as you see yourself.*

Step 3

1. Focus

When you have finished, talk with your partner about the thoughts and feelings you had as you completed the checklist. Which skills do you need to develop? How can you work on these skills in your relationship today? Which skills have you already developed well? Please remember to follow the guidelines for discussion outlined in section **a.** of this chapter.

When we are talking together, I focus my attention on you and what you are saying. I take the time to set everything else aside in order to hear you.

Rarely			Sometimes			Often
1	2	3	4	5	6	7

2. Responsibility

I recognize my thoughts, feelings, and opinions as my own, not the truth. I show this in statements that begin with "I." For example: "I think...," "I feel...," "I like..." rather than "You should...," "You make me feel...," "You never give me..."

Rarely			Sometimes			Often
1	2	3	4	5	6	7

3. Directness

I let you know in a straightforward way what I think and feel, even if it may result in conflict. I ask for what I want. I avoid sarcasm, teasing, lecturing, or distraction.

Rarely			Sometimes			Often
1	2	3	4	5	6	7

4. Listening

I listen carefully when you are talking. I listen to your words and feelings. I ask for clarification if I don't understand. I suspend my judgments. I seldom interrupt you.

Rarely			Sometimes			Often
1	2	3	4	5	6	7

5. Understanding

I let you know what I think you are saying and feeling. I respond by acknowledging your thoughts and feelings. I don't assume beforehand that I know what you think and feel.

Rarely			Sometimes			Often
1	2	3	4	5	6	7

6. Positive regard

I respect you as a person and show this to you. I appreciate your uniqueness in ideas, feelings, and experiences. I show you that I want you to be all you can be.

Rarely			Sometimes			Often
1	2	3	4	5	6	7

7. Self-disclosure

I openly express what I think, feel, and want. I tell you my fantasies. I can talk about my strengths and weaknesses, even those that might embarrass me. I let you know what is really happening with me.

Rarely			Sometimes			Often
1	2	3	4	5	6	7

8. Immediacy

I tell you, on a day-to-day basis, what I think and feel about the way we relate. I tell you what I like and don't like about how we relate. I want you to do this too.

Rarely			Sometimes			Often
1	2	3	4	5	6	7

9. Realism

I recognize you have your own thoughts, feelings, and attitudes. I can disagree without trying to change you or your viewpoint. I accept our differences.

Rarely			Sometimes			Often
1	2	3	4	5	6	7

10. Goodwill/respect

I say what I think, feel, and want without trying to intimidate or manipulate you. I care about you and your priorities as much as my own. I want you to be assertive even if we disagree.

Rarely			Sometimes			Often
1	2	3	4	5	6	7

Nancy: Well I'm so discouraged, I feel like I can't pull the images out of my head. But yes, tell me again what you said, I wasn't listening. Maybe it will help me stop my self-destructive pattern.

When Nancy really took in Ron's feedback, she was able to see her work from a different point of view and was inspired to continue.

1. Ask and you shall receive

The process of giving, asking for, and receiving feedback is one of the key components in intimate relationships. It is through feedback that you learn to see yourself as others see you. Through an effective exchange of feedback you create an atmosphere of caring, trust, acceptance, openness, and a concern for the needs of your loved one. Giving and receiving feedback is a skill that can be learned and developed, and for which certain useful guidelines exist.

The term "feedback" is borrowed from engineering. It refers to the process of taking information from the surrounding environment, feeding it into a device for measurement, and using those calibrated measurements to gauge how the machine should best respond to particular environmental changes. A thermostat is an example of a feedback mechanism. It gauges the temperature in the room and regulates the operation of the furnace based on the desired room temperature set by you.

A relationship can also be seen as a feedback instrument, with each partner sending agreed-upon signals to the other that indicate when the interaction is becoming "too hot," "too cold," or when everything is "just right." For example, your goal may be to become more aware of how your behavior affects your partner. Information from your partner can help you know whether you are moving toward your goal. If you react to negative feedback about your behavior by getting angry or leaving the room, you will not reach your goal. The relationship will become uncomfortably cool. Your partner can try to help you by saying, "You've asked me to tell you when your behavior irks me, but every time I give you feedback, you get angry and tell me I'm wrong. When you do this I don't want to talk to you any more. If you continue this behavior you won't reach your goal."

If you respond to the feedback by being more open to it next time, you will probably begin to get what you want. The result will be that you will feel better about yourself and your partner will warm up to you too. Feedback, then, is a technique that helps you get what you want in a relationship. It is also a way of comparing your own perceptions of your behavior with others' perceptions.

Giving feedback is a conscious verbal or nonverbal process by which you let others know what you are thinking or feeling about their behavior. The number one rule about giving feedback is *never ever give feedback unless the person asks for it or agrees to receive it*. Unwanted feedback always falls on deaf ears. It helps to use the following statement: "I have something to say to you. Are you willing to hear it?"

We consider giving feedback to be a *conscious* activity because it is something you choose to do. If you deliberately choose to give it, you are likely to take responsibility for the consequences that may follow. If your feedback is *unconscious,* you are emitting feedback (which is often referred to as bitching, complaining, or nagging), not giving it. You are also not likely to take responsibility for the consequences of your emissions. The result is that you will be puzzled by people's reactions to you.

When *asking for, soliciting* or *agreeing to receive* feedback, you want to know what others think and feel about *your* behavior; you agree to genuinely consider what the other has to say. Or, as Virginia Satir, the world famous family therapist says, "You agree to roll it around in your mouth to get a good taste of it before you spit out or swallow it wholeheartedly."

2. Intention versus behavior

When giving feedback you need to examine your intentions. Is your intention to inform, to hurt, or to manipulate? When receiving feedback you can never know the other person's intentions. You can only see his or her behavior. If you are in doubt about the intentions, ask. The assumption here, of course, is that the person will be truthful. If you assume anything else the exchange will be meaningless.

One of the most difficult and confusing aspects of couples' communications is that they tend to give feedback about each other's intentions, rather than their behaviors. For example, Jim comes home from work angry after having a fight with his boss. He starts slamming doors. Judy yells at him, "Just because I wasn't interested in sex last night isn't an excuse for being a boor today." That, of course, is like trying to put out a fire with gasoline. An explosion follows. Rather than focusing on Jim's behavior, Judy made an interpretation about his *intentions*. It would have been more productive for her to say, "You seem angry, what's going on?" Jim could then explain. Or, if he reacted angrily to her question she could say, "I don't know what you're angry about. When you're finished being angry I'll talk to you, but not before."

Confusion is added because many couples interpret each others' behavior as being negatively intended, when in fact it is not. It is often difficult to accept that your partner's intentions may not be what you assume them to be. *When in doubt, check it out with your partner.* For example, say something like, "When you said I should have checked the bank balance, were you telling me I am stupid?" Partner replies, "No, I was stating my opinion about how you might have avoided the mistake."

With this kind of exchange a more satisfying outcome is likely.

3. Responsibility: Who owns what?

In many feedback exchanges, the question of ownership arises. How much responsibility should the giver assume for his behavior and the receiver for her response? If Frank behaves in a way that evokes a negative response from Sara, how much ownership should each assume for their part of the interaction? Some people are willing to take on more than their share of the responsibility for their partner's responses. Others refuse to own any responsibility at all for their behavior.

For example, Frank has been coming home late three nights out of five for the last month. Sara starts giving him feedback about his lateness. His response is to point out that she's being a nag. He says he needs his freedom, he feels cramped, and that Sara is burdening him with too much responsibility. He doesn't understand why she wants him to be on time all the time, after all he's not a little boy.

The situation presents a dilemma for Sara. Her observations are accurate, but his reactions are provocative. One way she can clarify her dilemma is to point out that, while he certainly has a right to his freedom, the way he's going about it is going to have a negative effect on their relationship. To the extent that he cares about her and their relationship, he must consider her feedback.

Concern for your needs and the needs of others is a crucial element in the exchange of feedback. In a relationship you must not only be willing to take responsibility for your behavior, but you also have to be aware that your behavior has consequences.

4. Guidelines for giving and receiving feedback

Regardless of how accurate the feedback may be, if your partner does not accept the information, for whatever reason, the feedback is useless. Your feedback must be given so as to increase the probability that the person for whom it is intended can hear it in the most objective and least distorted way possible, understand it, and choose to use it or not use it.

EXAMPLE

Jill arrives home from a tough day at the office and finds Bob sitting reading the paper. Intending to be humorous, she says, "Boy, I wish I could be lazy like you." Bob responds, "You never let up, do you? I can't even sit and relax for a minute without your being on my back." Jill becomes angry and retaliates, and both people engage in the battle of who-can-hurt-whom-the-most.

Instead, Bob might give Jill feedback by stating his position in another way. That is, he could say, "I've had a rough day and I'm in a bad mood. When you said that to me I got my back up. Were you criticizing me or just trying to be funny?" This latter exchange is likely to have more effective results that the first.

Following are some guidelines that have proven effective in giving and receiving feedback.

(a) Direct versus indirect expression of thoughts and feelings

If Tracy says to Andy, "I love you," she is expressing her feelings directly, risking rejection or deepening of the relationship. However, if she is indirect and says, "You're such a lovable person," the risk of rejection is lessened, but so is the possibility of Andy reciprocating his love.

Indirect expression of thoughts and feelings is safer because it is ambiguous. Andy might guess that Tracy loves him, but Tracy can always deny it. If Andy rejects Tracy by saying, "I'm happy to hear that you think I'm a lovable person, but I do not love you," Tracy can counter, "You are a lovable person, but I don't love you either." When you express your thoughts and feelings indirectly, you are backing off from commitment. Direct expression means making a commitment to which your partner can respond directly and clearly. You wind up knowing exactly where you stand with the other.

"Why do you always drive so fast?" is an indirect expression of a feeling and a thought. The direct way to say it is "I get anxious when you drive fast (expresses feeling), I would really appreciate it if you would slow down (expresses thought)." Indirect statements often begin with "I feel that...," or "You are...," or "Why do you...?" and finish with an opinion. For example, "I feel that you are bored," or, "You're angry" are judgments, not feelings. They do not state what "I" is feeling. However, "I'm concerned (expresses a feeling) because I think you're bored and that you think I'm a boring person," or "I am anxious (expresses a feeling) because I think you're angry at me" states the speaker's positions directly.

A rule of thumb is that, nine times out of ten, a question is an indirect expression of a thought of feeling. Anytime you find yourself asking a question, rephrase it into a statement that expresses your thoughts or feeling directly.

(b) Interpretation versus description

Often couples do not understand a particular behavior of their partner and attach a motive to it in order to make sense out of it. When you attribute a motive to behavior you are interpreting that person's intention. Since your partner's intentions are only known to himself or herself, you need to find out whether or not your interpretations are accurate. This is particularly important in relationships because your interpretations arise out of attitudes that may not be shared by your partner.

EXAMPLE

Nick and Julianne have what they describe as a good sex life. They were making love late one night when, just as Nick was getting really turned on, he noticed that Julianne had fallen asleep. Nick rolled away to the other side of bed in a huff saying loudly, "You sure know how to put a guy down don't you!" which awoke the somewhat embarrassed Julianne.

Nick is interpreting Julianne's behavior. His attitude is that a woman should be interested in sex no matter how tired she may be. And furthermore, to turn a man down after getting him going is to put him down. His attitudes may create a distance between them or act as a bridge to a deeper understanding between them. He could have said after gently awaking Julianne, "You fell asleep in the middle of our lovemaking (description of behavior), I don't understand (self-disclosure), would you please tell me what's going on (direct request)?" Julianne may interpret her own behavior by saying, "I felt tired but I didn't realize how exhausted I was. When you began to caress me I completely relaxed and fell into a deep sleep. I like making love with you but I think I'm too tired tonight." In the morning Nick could talk with Julianne about his attitudes to masculinity that he learned as he was growing up and how that sometimes affects his feelings toward her.

Any time you interpret another's behavior or ascribe motives to it, the person tends to get defensive. He or she will feel a pressure to explain or rebelliously defend himself or herself. When you simply describe the behavior, your partner has an opportunity to make use of the feedback by interpreting or making sense of his or her own behavior. The probability is that you will feel closer to each other because you've engaged in dialogue, not battle.

(c) Nonjudgmental versus judgmental feedback

The most effective feedback is nonjudgmental. When you are giving feedback, you must respond to the person's behavior, not your estimation of her or his personal worth. When you tell your loved one that he is a boor or that she is an insensitive bitch it is not discussion. He may sometimes act like a Neanderthal or she may behave like a shrew, but that does not mean that either one of you is a completely stupid or insensitive person. When you evaluate your partner like that you put yourself in the role of a judge and place your partner in the role of the convicted person. It is difficult for anyone to respond to judgmental feedback because it offends his or her feelings of self-esteem. Besides, there is no way to respond once one has been "tried and convicted."

Direct, nonjudgmental feedback about boorishness might go like this: "When you touch me roughly (description of behavior) I get scared (feeling) and want to run away from you (self-disclosure). I would like you to touch me more gently and softly, like this (she would show him exactly how she likes to be touched)." To the charge of "insensitive bitch," a nonjudgmental approach would be, "I feel awful when you turn me down sexually (self-disclosure of feeling). I feel rejected. I don't know what to do or what you want (self-disclosure). I would appreciate it if you would tell me (direct request, expressed with common courtesy)."

(d) Specific versus general feedback

General feedback tends to create confusion because what you say can be interpreted in many different ways. When you give specific feedback you make a clear statement to the person about what specific behaviors you like or don't like as well as the consequence of those behaviors. With specific feedback there is little chance of misinterpretation.

EXAMPLE

Roger walks in from work, sees a mess in the family room, which is always untidy at the end of the day, and starts yelling at the kids. Karin, from the kitchen, comments, "Geez, you're hostile." Her feedback to him is given in general terms, and Roger might not know to which behavior she was referring. The term "hostile" does not specify what evoked a response in Karin. It would be more effective to say, "I hear you yelling at the kids for no good reason. I think you're angry at something. I would like to talk with you about it." If he says, "Yes," then they can go ahead. If he says, "No," then Karin will have to be specific in her request for a change in his behavior. She could say, "I do think you're angry. It seems to me that you're taking your frustrations out on the kids and I don't want you to do that because they wind up feeling badly about themselves and you. Then later you'll wonder why they are hesitant to approach you." Karin's feedback is specific. Roger knows exactly what behavior she is responding to, which he can change or modify.

(e) Freedom of choice versus pressure to change

When Karin told Roger about his behavior and the probable impact of it on his relationship with the children, she did not tell him he had to change. If his relationship with the children and Karin are important to Roger, however, he would consider the feedback and make the necessary changes. If they are not important to him, he might decide not to change.

It is essential that each individual in a relationship *experience the freedom* to use feedback in a meaningful way without thinking that they are required to change. When the giver of feedback tells or implies that the partner must change, he or she is assuming that he or she knows the correct standards for right and wrong or good and bad. When couples impose their own standards on each other, a great amount of resistance and resentment grows. The result is that the relationship becomes like a jail with each of the partners seeing the other as the jailer. All sense of personal responsibility is lost and each blames the other for almost everything.

But what if you keep giving your partner feedback about something you don't like and he or she persists in the behavior? You might exclaim, "What am I supposed to do? He won't change!" The most you can do is confront your partner with the consequences. Your partner cannot expect you to feel positive about him or her while also behaving in a way that you find irritating.

EXAMPLE

Lori is consistently late getting ready for the theater. Ken likes to be on time and has told her about his frustration many times but still waits for her while burning up inside. Usually they argue on the way as he tries to bully her into changing, which, of course, solidifies her resolve. To break the pattern Ken must give up trying to change Lori while outlining the consequences to her. He might say, "I am leaving at 7:30 for the play. I want to be with you but I am no longer going to wait for you."

No one can force you to change against your will — you can only change yourself. You may feel you have changed only to keep the peace, and blame your partner accordingly. But you are in total control of your own actions, even though you may not feel you are.

For lasting change to occur, the motivation for change has to come from within yourself. If you feel that the change has been imposed by your partner, resentment is sure to follow. One of the greatest expressions of love is to freely and willingly make a change in your behavior at the request of your partner, *while taking full responsibility for this decision to change*. Such change must be wholehearted and without reservations or expectations of receiving anything in return. An unexpected by-product of your chosen changes is that your partner is likely to change in relationship to you.

(f) Immediate versus delayed timing

To be most effective, feedback should, whenever possible, be given immediately following the event. If you wait too long to give feedback, the receiver may not remember the situation or your recollection of the event may become clouded. You may get into arguments over details and the original intention of the feedback may be lost. This doesn't mean that you need to give the feedback in front of the dinner guests, for example, but soon after they leave is probably the best time.

We end each day with what we call *clearing*. We set aside 10 to 15 minutes for *appreciations*, which are things we liked about our day and each other, and *resentments*, which include things we didn't like about our day or things one of us did that the other didn't like. We also say whatever is on our minds, both positive and negative, before we go to bed. By clearing on a daily basis we keep our relationship up to date, fresh, interesting, and alive.

We also recommend that couples plan an open, regularly scheduled feedback session for one hour, twice a week. During this time you agree to give each other feedback about how you think your relationship is going. It's also an opportunity for each of you to talk about how satisfied you are with yourself, separate from the relationship.

You might talk about your hopes, dreams, fears, and the things you feel good about. Perhaps you might ask your partner for his or her impressions of you these days. This activity is frightening for most couples in the beginning, but the more you do it the more it can become a valuable, exciting aspect of your relationship.

In the section on self-disclosure, you had an opportunity to assess your relationship skills. The following activity is designed to help you assess your partner's skills plus learn how to give feedback to each other more effectively.

Working separately, go through the list below. Circle one of the numbers under each skill described that best expresses the way you see your partner.

1. Focus

When I am talking with you, you focus your attention on me and what I am saying. You take the time to set everything else aside in order to hear me.

Rarely		Sometimes			Often	
1	2	3	4	5	6	7

2. Responsibility

You recognize your thoughts, feelings, and opinions as being your own, not *the* truth. You show this in statements that begin with "I." For example: "I think...," "I feel...," "I like..."

Rarely		Sometimes			Often	
1	2	3	4	5	6	7

3. Directness

You let me know, in a straightforward way, what you think and feel, even if it may result in conflict. I think you ask for what you want. You avoid sarcasm, hurtful teasing, lecturing me, or distractions.

Rarely		Sometimes			Often	
1	2	3	4	5	6	7

4. Listening

You listen carefully when I am talking. You listen to my words and feelings. You ask for clarification if you don't understand. You suspend your judgments. You seldom interrupt me when I'm talking with you.

Rarely		Sometimes			Often	
1	2	3	4	5	6	7

5. Understanding

You let me know what you think I am saying and feeling. You respond by acknowledging my thoughts and feelings. You don't assume beforehand that you know what I think and feel. I think you understand me.

Rarely		Sometimes			Often	
1	2	3	4	5	6	7

6. Positive regard

I think you respect me as a person. You show this to me. I feel that you appreciate my uniqueness in ideas, feelings, and experiences. You show me that you want me to be all I can be.

Rarely		Sometimes			Often	
1	2	3	4	5	6	7

7. Self-disclosure

You openly express to me what you think, feel, and want. You tell me about your hopes and dreams. I see you as being willing to talk about your strengths and weaknesses that might embarrass you. I feel you let me know what is really happening to you.

Rarely			Sometimes			Often
1	2	3	4	5	6	7

8. Immediacy

You tell me what you think and feel about the way we relate. You tell me how you see us in the present. I think you tell me what you like and don't like about how we relate.

Rarely			Sometimes			Often
1	2	3	4	5	6	7

9. Realism

I believe you accept that I have my own thoughts, feelings and attitudes. You can disagree without trying to change me or my viewpoint. I think you can accept our differences.

Rarely			Sometimes			Often
1	2	3	4	5	6	7

10. Goodwill/respect

You say what you think, feel, and want without trying to intimidate or manipulate me. I think you care about me and my priorities as much as your own. I think you want me to be assertive even if we disagree.

Rarely			Sometimes			Often
1	2	3	4	5	6	7

When you have finished, talk with your partner about your rating. Follow the guidelines for giving and receiving feedback. You will require at least one hour of uninterrupted time to do this.

5

PLEASE HEAR WHAT I'M SAYING

When two people live together, share meals, juggle career and home life, make love, raise children, deal with in-laws, witness their individual ups and downs, and hold joint bank accounts, the quality of their lives is greatly determined by how well they communicate and manage conflict.

In previous chapters you have already had an opportunity to begin to learn some communications skills: self-disclosure, giving and receiving feedback, and listening. In this chapter you will have an opportunity to learn how to communicate more effectively so that the day-to-day conflicts that occur in relationships can actually bring you and your partner closer together. We will also examine more deeply how couples communicate, what they do effectively, and what kinds of behaviors interfere with the communication process.

EXAMPLE

One evening Joyce arrived home late from work, stomped into the house with a grunted greeting, shouted at her children about watching too much television, and shot a few sarcastic remarks at her husband, John. Instead of reacting angrily to her foul mood, John looked at her softly, slid up beside her and gently asked what was going on. After a couple more verbal jabs, which John did not take personally, Joyce eventually revealed that she had the worst day at work in her entire life and is now afraid that her boss thinks she's incom-

petent. She talked about her frustration about not having more responsibility in her job. In the next few minutes, Joyce shared her career ambitions and goals, and admitted to some fears and hopes that she had never told him before. John offered no advice, but simply acknowledged that he understood and supported her. In this case, a potential fight was averted and the couple arrived at a new level of sharing and intimacy.

a. THE IMPORTANCE OF COMMUNICATION SKILLS

The basic, most important skills that you must possess to deal effectively with interpersonal problems are communication skills. This is screamingly obvious to anyone who has ever been in a long-term relationship. Every book that has ever been written about relationships emphasizes that communication skills are necessary to long-lasting love and happiness. The first thing that a couple who is having problems will say is, "We don't communicate anymore!" Even the business world is beginning to wake up to the importance of developing good interpersonal communications. *In Search of Excellence*, which has sold more copies than any other business book, emphasizes again and again the importance of interpersonal communications.

Every couple, at one time or another, faces difficult and stressful issues. A *successful relationship* is one that, when faced with difficulties, draws upon the resources of both individuals, and becomes stronger; their love for each other deepens through this process. Relationships fail when, having been confronted with problems, one or both of the individuals does not have the resources or is unwilling to use available resources. As a result, one or both of the partners feels weaker or less capable of dealing with life's problems, and in the long run, one or both of them feels distant from the other.

In other words, successful relationships are not without their difficulties, but both partners are willing to work toward finding solutions to their problems. We may be belaboring this point but it is one which people seem unable to acknowledge. This is due in large part to the myth that successful, happy people do not have problems, which is reinforced daily in advertisements, TV, and celebrity shows. Generally, our society's attitude is that if you have personal problems you're either stupid or bad.

If most couples communicated naturally, the rate of divorce, unhappiness, and violence in relationships would be drastically reduced. But most couples do not communicate naturally. *Communications skills must be continuously learned and practiced and practiced and practiced.* Communications skills are the foundation of relationships. As in a building, if the foundation is weak it must be repaired or the building will eventually fall down, no matter what you do to the upper structure. If the foundation is strong and well maintained, the structure can be blown apart but you can start to rebuild on the same foundation the next day.

The desire for a relationship is alive and well. People do want to find love, understanding, and companionship. But these qualities of relationship must be learned and earned. Learning how to communicate effectively is the place to start. To assess your skill as a communicator, work through Activity #11.

b. THE FIVE KEY ELEMENTS IN COMMUNICATING

Communication is the process of exchanging desires, needs, and feelings as well as facts and ideas. The key elements in any act of communication are the sender and receiver of the message, the form of the message, the content, and the intent.

1. The sender and receiver

For our purposes, the sender and receiver are the partners in a relationship. An exchange does not take place unless one sends a message and the other receives it. The effectiveness of the exchange is determined by the physiological and psychological condition of the individuals as well as the perceived relationship between a couple.

EXAMPLE

Frank comes home from work late and Sally is miffed.

Sally: You're late again!

Frank: Yeah, I guess so. (He walks into the other room to pour himself a drink.)

Sally: You could have at least called?!

Frank: I tried! The line was busy...as usual! (Silence)

Sally: You could at least say you're sorry!

Frank: All right, all right, I'm sorry. Are you happy now?!

There are 38 words spoken in the exchange in the above example. It might have lasted 5, maybe even 10 minutes. In that short space of time Frank and Sally have set the scene for an evening of protracted, unpleasant tension. A lonely gulf exists between them. Tied up in that brief exchange is a wealth of information about these two personalities, their feelings of self-esteem,

ACTIVITY #11
COMMUNICATION SELF-ASSESSMENT

Answer each statement by writing in the number that best describes the statement as it applies to you over the last few months.

       1. Never true
       2. Hardly ever
       3. Sometimes
       4. Almost always
       5. Always true

_____ I like talking with my partner in one-to-one conversations
_____ I include my partner in small group conversations
_____ I willingly talk with my partner about issues we are in conflict about
_____ My partner tells me I am easy to talk with
_____ I include myself in small group conversations when my partner is present
_____ My partner tells me his or her problems
_____ I let my partner know how and when I appreciate him or her
_____ I listen to my partner when she or he talks
_____ My partner tells me I communicate well
_____ I feel my partner understands me
_____ I am able to clearly get my ideas across to my partner
_____ TOTAL

The higher you score (out of a possible total of 55) the better you can communicate with your partner. If you score 30 or less, you should ask your partner to go with you to a couples communication program so you can learn to communicate better with her or him.

their attitudes toward one another, their memories of past conversations, their "unwritten rules" about communication, and the current stage of their relationship (probably resignation).

How we interpret any message coming from another person will be governed by our entire life history of interpersonal communications as well as the immediate circumstances, surrounding the exchange. We make *assumptions* about the sender's intended message based on the content of the words, the tone in which they are spoken, and the physical context in which the words are uttered. For example, if Jill comes home and cheerfully says, "Hi, how are you?" and her husband, Paul, sitting in the chaise lounge absorbed in a pile of papers, replies almost absentmindedly, "Fine, dear," Julie *assumes* from his posture that he is concentrating on studying for his exam tomorrow and does not want to be disturbed. He conveyed his message not so much through his words as his body language. If Jill has had a particularly bad day and her self-esteem is low, she might *assume* that he doesn't care about her, and she might get angry at him. Or, if Paul's lack of response causes Jill to remember her similarly non-responsive father, she may feel anxiety and give up on trying to talk to him for the rest of the evening. The first rule is CHECK OUT THE ASSUMPTIONS THAT YOU ARE MAKING ABOUT YOUR PARTNER.

The purpose of communication is to increase understanding between people and to create a desire for continuing the exchange. The best communication is like two people having a friendly, leisurely game of catch. The ball is tossed back and forth in a way that makes it as easy as possible for each person to catch. As they become more proficient, the two can mutually agree to test their skills by moving further apart or by delivering the ball more forcefully — the intention being to deepen interest, not create competition. Afterward the two feel much closer.

The worst communication is like an extremely competitive tennis match with no referees. The two serve one another backhands deflected with topspin or blistering forehands which are difficult to return. They argue, pout, and rant over whether the balls are in or out. The loser is deflated; the "winner" feels powerful. They're both exhausted.

2. Form of the message

A message can be conveyed in words or in silence, with shouts or tears, in a giggle or a caress. A rigid posture can send as powerful a message as a few well-chosen words; so can a grimace, a smile, a well-timed yawn, or a paternal pat on the head. A message can also be communicated in writing: in a scrawled note on the kitchen bulletin board, "Won't be home for supper tonight," or in a love letter punctuated with "P.S. I love you."

The same words can have dramatically different meanings depending on the tone of voice they are delivered with. If Sam asks calmly and in a friendly, inquisitive tone, "Where's the paper?," Carol will probably *assume* that he is just asking for information and the exchange will proceed smoothly. But if he angrily demands, "Where's the paper?," she might *assume* that he is implying, "You idiot! You moved the paper from my usual spot. You're a bother in my life!"

A mixed message is one in which your words contradict your actions or body language. Sara says, "No, of course I'm not angry," but then sits in rigid, cold silence. She is sending a mixed message. She is not admitting her anger, but is showing it nevertheless. When a man tells his wife he loves her, then proceeds to ignore her wishes that they spend more time talking together, he is sending mixed messages. Often our words are a cover for our real, deeper feelings. This is especially true when we fear (assume) that expressing the emotion directly will have unpleasant consequences. A rule of thumb is *go by the person's actions, not his or her words.* In any event, check out your assumptions.

3. Content

The content of a message can do four things:

(a) It can convey a message: "I took your laundry in today, it will be ready Friday." "The magazine is in the bedroom."

(b) A message can transmit a feeling. To do this most clearly the feeling should be bodily expressed: "I'm angry" (expressed seriously and with lifted voice). "I feel sad" (if deep enough, accompanied by tears). "I love you" (followed by a warm hug).

(c) A message can convey the desire to have a power or authority over the other. It may be aimed at controlling the other: "You should..." "Get the door, would you!?" "No child of mine is going out like that!"

(d) A message can make a statement about your values, beliefs, dreams, prejudices, or outlook on life: "What's the use?" (If said often can reveal a chronic depression.) "Men only want one thing from women." (I don't enjoy sex with you anymore).

4. Intent

Clear communication requires that you be aware of your intent. Are you entering into this exchange to create more understanding, love, and intimacy? Or are you more interested in controlling the other, getting your own way, or making your partner feel bad, guilty, or stupid?

If your intent is to control your partner, get your own way, or make him or her feel bad, guilty, or stupid, then your partner is likely to become defensive and your ex-

changes will lead to more conflict. Your partner will eventually stop talking to you. If your intent is to create more understanding, love, and intimacy, your partner is going to remain open to what you have to say. In the long run your communications will become more satisfying.

c. THE ROLE OF LANGUAGE

Language is part of our very being. We give meaning to all our experiences through language. To say, "It was so fantastic I cannot describe it!" is an attempt to render meaning to a profound experience. The listener will not know the experience but will have a greater appreciation of the other's reactions to the experience. Without the words the other is left to conjecture.

Language, and how it is served up, is only a tool for making connections. It is a way of creating images in people's minds as well as a method of reaching a person's internal feelings. Leo Bascaglia, Jane Fonda, Ronald Reagan, and Gloria Steinem all use language to inspire or infuriate. Your understanding of language depends on internal images you associate with their words and how they are delivered.

Because language is so important it is crucial that each person develop linguistic skills to communicate clearly with others. Unfortunately, some of the most important words cannot be absolutely defined because they are primitive and subject to individual interpretation. Some examples are the words mother, joy, freedom, life, father, love, sex, money, companionship, happiness. Ask 100 people to define those words and you'll get 100 different definitions.

In relationships these words need to be talked about so that women and men can arrive at a better understanding of themselves and each other. The degree to which people in relationships misunderstand basic words is the degree to which they are unaware of themselves.

Recently there has been much written about the importance of the nonverbal aspects of interpersonal communications. Some people go around "reading" their partner's body language, thinking they "know" what is happening with the other. But it is all based on speculation. What is really going on when you "read" another's body language is that you become aware of your own assumptions about the other's behavior. You may be right, but you could also be wrong. The only way to know the purpose of the other's behavior is to have a conversation about the assumption you are making about that person's nonverbal behavior. Through the conversation the dynamics of your relationship will become clearer; you will feel closer to or more distant from the person and you are likely to understand why.

The only way for one human being to know accurately what is going on in another's mind is through the exchange of words. All else is speculative at best and moralistic at worst. Additionally, one of the most effective ways of finding out what's going on within yourself is to have a conversation with a trusted and loyal friend or counselor.

The most important change you can make in your language is to use the word "I," not "you," when speaking about yourself. Often, people generalize their statements by using "you," which is a way of avoiding responsibility for their feelings. They use "you" to mean "everybody," but they are really talking about themselves. For example, Dan might say to Fred, "When you try to explain something to Susan, you get really nervous." What Dan really means is "When I try to explain something to Susan, I get really nervous." The second statement is clear. The use of "I" when you are talking about yourself is one powerful, direct behavior that will clarify your communications. When you use "I," you become connected with your internal experience and it is clear to others what you are trying to say. Reserve "you" for referring to others.

Language can distance you not only from other people but from yourself as well. If you use "ownership language" you can understand yourself better, be more integrated, and communicate with others more clearly. Some examples of ownership language versus non-ownership language are given below.

Non-ownership language

That feels good.

It hurts.

You hurt me.

You make me feel good.

Ownership language

I feel good.

I hurt.

I hurt when you say that.

I feel good when I'm with you.

Couples often will speak of "we" when relating experiences or feelings. In verbal communication the use of "we" makes the assumption that "I" can speak for the other and may cut off dialogue and create misunderstandings. For example, you might say, "When we fight we don't listen." Your partner might disagree, saying, "*I* listen but I think *you* don't listen to me, so don't include me in that statement." Our rule of thumb is that *we never refer to "we" unless we've talked about it and have agreed openly on the particular issue that one of us is talking about.*

Another subtle behavioral pattern that couples have is talking *about* the partner when he or she should be talked *to*. If a partner is present, it is respectful, straightforward, and efficient to talk *to*, not *about*, him or her. For example, instead of saying, "That's what he says when he's angry," say, "That's what you say when you're angry at me."

Generally women are more proficient verbally in intimate encounters than men.

Men often feel inept when it comes to the give and take of lively heterosexual conversations. Men often charge women with, "You talk too much!" or "You women are always analyzing things to death." Women accuse men of being inaccessible because men are reluctant to talk about their thoughts, feelings, or internal states. In our experience, when both are communicating well, an equal exchange takes place.

One final note about language is that if it isn't working, drop it. If you find yourself saying the same thing over and over again to your partner, but you don't feel heard, give up. There's no use trying to beat a dead horse. How often have you heard yourself saying for the hundredth time, "If things don't change around here soon, that's it, I'm leaving." Don't waste your breath, it's time for action. Or, how often have both of you talked about how you should make love more often — but then don't. The next time you find yourselves talking about it, take a risk and do it.

d. THE PRESSURE OF TIME

Practically every study on family stress ranks time pressures near the top. Almost every couple who comes to see us for counseling says, "We should have done something about our relationship years ago." Most people would say that they should work less. We have conducted a study of two-career couples and discovered that the typical Monday to Friday week for each person follows this pattern:

40 hours spent on the job

10 hours commuting

5 hours lunch (we consider this time to be work oriented since the person's time is restricted)

5 hours getting ready for work

5 hours to wind down from work (after a good day, longer if you have a bad day)

This totals 65 hours of work-related time per week, or 12.4 hours per day. Add 10 hours (minimum) per week to the woman's time if there is one child; add 18 hours (minimum) per week to the woman's time if there are two children.

Most men, in the opinion of women, do not contribute much to the care and feeding of the children. This is especially true if the man is ambitious in his career. If the man is genuinely helpful around the house, the two may work the same number of hours and both will feel less strained because they're "in this together." This perception goes a long way to relieving a couple's interpersonal stress.

The schedule shown above leaves little time for what most people say is most important to them: time with their partners, children, friends, and self. When a couple doesn't take enough time to be together without distractions, communication suffers. When communication suffers, couples are less able to deal with day-to-day issues. Arguments break out over seemingly trivial things, which adds more stress and uneasiness between partners. This, in turn, leads to each avoiding the other, further compounding the time problem. Estrangement or affairs are the probable consequences.

Many couples develop creative ways for finding time for self, partner, family, and friends. How do they do it? They use the following guidelines.

1. Heartbeats are a non-renewable resource

We are given a certain number of heartbeats in our lifetime. Nobody knows how many; it's different for each person. Ask yourself this question: "Is what I'm doing right now the way I want to expend my heartbeats, knowing that they can never be recovered?" This is another way of saying that time is finite and as with any limited resource it must be controlled carefully. Think of the last year of your life and how quickly it has gone by. You are now one year older. You have one year less to live. It may be a morbid thought to many people but most people treat their time as if there is no end to it.

Controlling your time requires planning. It means sitting down together and going over weekly and long-range calendars. You must plan the amount of time you will take in the upcoming week to eat meals together and to relax. If your schedule looks impossibly full, and if you value your relationship, you will eliminate some extraneous activities. If you pay attention to your time now you can avoid future time pressures and the inevitable communication problems.

Most people dislike the thought of planning and complain that it takes too much time. But there is no way out; if you don't take charge of your time, it, along with you and your relationship, will slip away into history. We all make promises to ourselves to do the important things once the present emergency is over. But emergencies, crises, and projects have a way of following one on the other, eating away quality time together. That is one major reason why so many relationships fall apart.

Making decisions about how to use your time requires courage. It isn't easy to say to a friend or relative, "Sorry, but we can't spend time with you right now because our relationship comes first." Most people don't do this. They invite guests over, allow friends to drop in at any time, give in to the pressures of work responsibilities, and get too involved in their families. Then they end up blaming others rather than themselves.

2. Home versus office: The vital balance

When work becomes the primary focus of either partner's life, breakdowns in communication are inevitable. Successful couples don't let work intrude on their family life. They make an agreement to call each other's attention to any neglect of family. Each also agrees that when the fact is pointed out the offending partner will change his or her behavior.

Organizations and businesses are, by their nature, almost completely concerned with survival and profitability. Most companies pay only lip service to the human needs of employees. An organization will take as much as an employee is willing to give, and make demands to the point of burning out its people. Professional training is designed to teach the apprentices to sacrifice themselves for the profession. This is particularly evident in those professions that have grueling periods of internship such as accounting, medicine, architecture, law, and all of the helping professions. For people in these professions, divorce or an unhappy home life seems to be a prerequisite for success. The

ACTIVITY #12
REFLECTION ACTIVITY

Take time to reflect on the following questions:

- Do you make your relationship a priority through your everyday words and actions?

- Does your partner?

- Do you take enough time for yourself?

- Do you often feel pressured for time?

- Can you say "No" to others' demands for your time?

self-employed also often seem willing to forego love for material success. The self-sacrificing work ethic is deeply embedded in our minds.

Only a courageous decision to take charge of your life will lead to personal fulfillment *and* material success. In our couples workshops we have a difficult time getting couples to realize that they can govern their own home and work life. Once they do take charge, there is an immediate and dramatic change in their relationship. Some people even change jobs when work demands cannot be reduced, as in those companies with an "up-or-out" policy.

EXAMPLES

1. Tom's boss would take every minute of his time if Tom didn't assert himself. Tom values the satisfaction of having a loving relationship as well as the pleasure and responsibilities of being a father. Because they both work, Tom and Marta meet together regularly to talk about how to balance home and office. They recognize that they are new to this two-career game and what they learned in their families doesn't work for them. They make sure that they take a minimum of 15 minutes in the morning and 30 minutes each evening to talk without being disturbed.

2. Gene said he used to resent Pamela, a teacher, for coming home exhausted after a day's teaching, then spending the evening going over papers or going to committee meetings. "We started to fight a lot, or alternatively, not talk for days. It finally took a crisis to wake us up." Gene had an affair. When he told Pamela, it certainly opened up communications. "We started paying attention to each other's needs. We worked out a satisfac-tory solution in which Pamela now does paperwork only a few times a week and we spend more time talking and relaxing together. We end our day with a little ritual that we use to get back in touch with each other. First, we share how we're feeling personally or what happened to us during the day that we felt good or bad about. Next, we exchange how we're feeling about each other or clear up any misunderstanding that may have arisen over a day or two. It's amazing how quickly we can get out of sync with each other. Finally, we talk about the tasks that we have to do separately or together so that we know what each of us is up to. Sometimes we just say, 'To heck with the work,' and go out to a movie, cuddle up on the couch together, go for a long walk, or make love. Since we've been doing it, our lives have been so satisfying and pleasurable, it's amazing."

Many people are now beginning to realize that the cost of material success is not worth the price. If you are feeling this way, you can begin getting back in touch with each other by doing the following activity.

e. MAKING CONTACT

One of the main benefits of establishing clear communication between couples is increased health and well-being. Dr. James Lynch of the University of Maryland School of Medicine has found that dramatic changes in heart rate and blood pressure take place during the course of couple's communication. Using computers to monitor blood pressure and other vital signs, Lynch observed the impact of communication. Blood pressure rises with speech and falls with listening. It rises to dangerous levels in those who already have high blood pressure. In an equal exchange the blood pressures level out to

ACTIVITY #13
THE ONE DAY DO-IT-YOURSELF RELATIONSHIP RENEWAL PROGRAM

Make an agreement to set aside one day just for the two of you. If you have children, arrange child care. If you want to stay in your home, arrange to have them go somewhere for the day. Take the phone off the hook. Tell your friends you will not be available at all during the appointed day. If someone drops in, resist the temptation to answer the door. Do not read, listen to the radio, watch TV, or play music, unless the music is used to enhance your contact. Leave all projects unfinished and all housework undone. Don't go shopping or on any outings, unless it's a leisurely walk. If you go away from home, say to a hotel, stay in the room, just being together. Agree to talk about your personal life only, not the kids, not work, not relatives, friends, or anything else that might detract from making an interpersonal connection. Don't talk about the practical problems in your life like money, whether to buy that new washer, or getting the car serviced. Stick to the personal and interpersonal. Don't pick a fight with your partner just because you're bored or uncomfortable. Let the silences be there, unless that is your usual way. If that is the case take turns talking about yourself and/or each other. Or, if one person is usually silent, that person can agree to do most of the talking during the day, while the other will concentrate on listening. Be creative and take risks. Have a pillow fight. Massage each other.

When you find that "it's not working" or that "it's a waste of time" to do this, that is exactly when you must stick with it through the rest of the day. Talk about those thoughts and feelings.

The next day spend some time alone reflecting on the day and writing out your thoughts, feelings, and impressions. Keep a record of these and review them together periodically.

Do this activity once a month for six months, and thereafter every three months. Set aside times in your calendar just as you would for any other important appointment.

lower, healthier levels. In another study it was found that if couples experience a growing closeness when they are communicating, their hearts begin to beat in unison.

Intimacy requires the presence of another person. That other person must be present physically, emotionally, and spiritually in order for contact to be established. Contact is hard to define, yet we all have a sense of when another person is truly with us or off in another world. Togetherness, companionship, closeness, intimacy, and friendship are words we use to describe the sensation of being in contact with another person. These sensations occur when two individuals make a conscious effort to move toward or open up to each other. Loneliness, isolation, coldness, withdrawal are the opposite of contact and the result of one or both people protecting themselves from the other.

Contact can be contrived to make it appear as though a connection is being made when in fact there is none. If both individuals collude in their contrivance, the result will be a relationship as empty and brittle as last year's blown Easter egg. If one person contrives contact while the other seeks it, the latter will feel empty, despairing, and at times a little "crazy." The source of the emptiness will be the dishonesty of the partner. The foundation of the despair will be in the inability to reach what appears to be real (i.e., the partner) but what, in fact, is an illusion. If you feel "crazy" in this kind of situation it's because any questioning about your partner's intentions is met with indignant denial. The only way to shatter the illusion is to trust your feelings about what is going on and not listen to your partner's words. Trusted and supportive friends are a great resource during those times.

Over the years couples can become almost completely out of contact with each other. When that occurs they often don't know how to begin communicating intimately again. Keeping in contact keeps the life blood of a relationship flowing. Activity #14 is a process for opening the lines of communication. It is the sentence completion technique from our *Marriage Survival Kit*.

f. HONESTY VERSUS TRUTH

Sometimes we get caught between honesty and truth. Our relationships get muddy. Our arguments go around in circles. We have hurtful fights with our partners without knowing why.

"I was just being honest!" or "That's what I really think, so why not say it?" or "Express your feelings!" is the dictum of the decade. Why don't you usually feel better after a round of screaming honesty? Being honest may not be the real you. It may be just the tip of the iceberg. Of course, honesty can be useful for clearing the surface rubble of years of lies. However, it is often only a first step toward a deeper truth.

Truth is the expression of thoughts, feelings, and actions that endure and connect with a deep part of you and *that respect another's sense of humanness*. In the development of satisfying, loving relationships you need to be aware of whether you are being honest or truthful. Honesty has a here-and-now value; truth represents something basic and enduring, something that brings meaning and unity to the past, present, and future. Truth helps you make sense of the past. It brings a feeling of being grounded in the present. It is the basis for making decisions that will determine how you create your future.

In every relationship, however affectionate, there's often an element of hostility — a lurking, primal urge to put the other down, to place him or her in the wrong, to make him or her feel guilty or bad. Usually we keep these urges in check. However, in the heat of battle we often express feelings or thoughts that are honest, but not completely true, in order to hurt or control the other. Some examples are phrases like, "I never should have married you!"; "You'll never amount to anything!"; "I've never enjoyed sex with you!"; "You disgust me!" These statements are usually the result of acute stress or anxiety in which all your fears explode to the surface. In a desperate attempt to regain control your words burst forth. You've scratched the surface, but have not yet reached the core of the truth.

The essential consideration in distinguishing between honesty and truth is whether your momentary feelings or thoughts recur and persist. Are your thoughts and feelings durable, or a reaction to a sudden perceived threat to your sense of self-esteem? Ask yourself, "What am I afraid of now? How do I feel threatened?"

Honesty often has the effect of separating people. Truth draws people closer if both people are willing to deal with the truth. Honesty and truth are related but

ACTIVITY #14
OPENING THE LINES OF COMMUNICATION

Set aside some time when the two of you can relax and be alone together without the possibility of any outside distractions. Do not use alcohol or any other drugs while doing this activity. You might put some soft, relaxing music on low volume. Sit opposite each other; decide who is going to start completing the sentences. Remember to listen and breathe. You may wish to record the conversation.

Take turns completing the following sentences. Say whatever comes to your mind.

The first time we met I thought you _____

_____

I was initially attracted to you because _____

_____

One way in which I think we are alike is _____

_____

One way in which I think we are different is _____

_____

Right now I'm feeling _____

_____

I get angry at you when _____

_____

Some of my needs that I am not fulfilling are _____

_____

In the last year I_____

_____

I assume you know that_____

_____

I get annoyed when I see you _____

_____

One of the ways I try to control you is _____

_____

When we have a serious discussion I _____

_____

Right now I'm feeling _____

_____

When I don't want to answer your questions, I_____

_____

Something I am usually reluctant to discuss with you is _____

_____

I feel inferior to you when _____

_____

To keep from being hurt by you I _____

_____

I become most defensive when I think you _____

_____

When we fight I feel _____

_____

I think you do not give me a chance to _____

_____

When I want to spite you, I _____

_____

I feel closest to you when_____

_____

A source of pain for me in this relationship is _____

_____

The kind of relationship I want to develop with you is _____

_____

In regard to this relationship, one thing I want you to do differently is _____

_____

I hope that we can_____

_____

_____

_____

_____

_____

_____

_____

basically different experiences and values. You are honest *and* true if what you say is consistent with your basic self. For example, I may honestly hate you at this moment; the truth is that I am terrified that you might leave me and I am afraid to tell you, so I say I hate you instead.

Why do we "lie" like this? Because very early in our upbringing we learn that the best defense is an explosive offense.

Honesty is a relative value; you say, "You're a cold bitch." Truth is self-reverential: "When I can't turn you on, I doubt my manhood. Then I hate myself for being incompetent. So I call you a cold bitch instead of facing the truth of my insecurities." Romantic love is honest: "You love me. I must be a good person. You love me. Therefore I am lovable. I love you, too." Love that undergoes the tests of time, crises, and changes, yet continues to grow is mature love: "When we first met, I thought I couldn't live without you. Now, I don't need you, and I want to be with you forever."

In relationships, a sudden burst of honesty is often a response to unacknowledged, unexpressed feelings. A blast of honesty can bring a breath of fresh air to an otherwise stale relationship. If nothing else it will add excitement to your interactions. Our advice to couples during the "honest" period is to listen, but don't take it personally. Honest anger may become compassion if you are seeking a level of truth that will bring satisfaction. For example, the *truth* of the statement, "I never should have married you," is, "I have been dissatisfied for many years now. I was too much of a coward to tell you of my dissatisfaction. I blamed you instead of facing the truth and doing something about it. I have been lying to myself and you all these years. I'm not going to do that anymore. I may come on heavy but it's the only way I know how to break out of my inertia of self-deception." This kind of truth, while painful for your partner, can be handled because it is grounded in reality. We human beings can deal with the most painful truths; it's the deceptions and lies that drive us crazy.

When confronting another person you must be aware of both your honest response at the moment and the long-range truth. They may be in conflict. Be aware of the choices you are making. If you are seeking the deepest level of communication, choose the enduring truth, not the momentary honesty. By expressing yourself in ways that lead to deeper levels of communication and self-awareness, you will find that you can be yourself while being in a relationship. In this light the truth will, indeed, set you free.

g. MAKING CHOICES

Learning how to communicate well with your partner does not mean you'll get everything you want. Couples who communicate clearly have to face making decisions and when we make a decision, we must, by necessity, say yes to one option and no to others. This is, of course, why many people keep communications unclear, so they will never have to choose. Obfuscation as an art form reaches its pinnacle in the realm of politics. If you and your partner are always trying to avoid making decisions, then your communications will be clouded and obscure.

What makes our choices difficult is not saying yes, but saying no. And yet it is the no that gives the yes meaning and power.

EXAMPLE

Gary has a relationship with two women: Janet and Karin. Matters are getting serious. He wants an intense and loyal relationship with one woman only. Both love him and he loves them. To say yes to both is easy. He could wait until one of them gets fed up and rejects him, thereby leaving him with only one "choice." But this path is fraught with disaster because Gary would not have made a real choice; he would know it and hate himself every time he was with the "leftover" one. The "leftover" would also know it and would lose respect for him and hate herself for allowing herself to be treated that way. The tough part of the choice Gary must make is that he must risk saying no. He wants to say yes to Karin, but that means saying no to Janet. Karin will be happy, but Janet will be deeply hurt and feel betrayed. That is difficult and painful for both her and him. If things go wrong with Karin, he will not be able to return to Janet. But by risking the pain, the anger, the rejection, and the loss involved in saying no to Janet, he demonstrates the seriousness of his commitment to Karin. His saying yes to Karin acquires credibility by means of his saying no to Janet.

Children, when asked to make choices, will characteristically always say yes. They do not possess the strength and the realism to say no. Parents have to make decisions for children. But this kind of situation is destructive to relationships between adults. You cannot choose for another person; an authentic choice can only be made by the individual. This is true even in joint decision making. The unwillingness to say no to a boss, a colleague, a doctor, a parent, a child, a lover, or a partner is tantamount to paralysis. If you refuse to say no and commit to yes, your life and your relationships will be kept in limbo. To act, to live, to love requires the mature willingness to say no and accept the consequences of commitment.

Some people *always* say no, which is the same as saying yes to everything. It reflects an unwillingness to risk commitment and it means that you are not willing to take full responsibility for the consequences of your decisions.

h. THE ART OF CONVERSATION

The biggest problem in most relationships is the frustration of not being able to talk together "the way you used to." One of you wants something from the other that you're not getting. But you don't ask, or if you do, you're not heard.

In today's fast-paced world the initial irritations of the proverbial seven-year itch begin to crop up in the second year of marriage. That's when you start to wonder what ever happened to those long interesting conversations over candlelit dinners the two of you once shared, or what became of the loving person with whom you could share everything. In the routine of everyday living, it is easy to let things go until you have a complete breakdown in communications. Successful couples have a very simple secret. When problems crop up, successful couples don't give up, they take time to sit down and talk about what has gone wrong and what needs to be done to make it right again. Then they do what is necessary to make it happen. They know how to use the dynamics of the art of conversation.

Conversation is a way of exchanging information between people with a view to solving problems or simply making contact. It involves feelings, thoughts, and action. Figure #6 graphically illustrates the five-step process of successful conversations. The steps are represented in a circular diagram to show that communication is a continuous, fluid, back-and-forth process. The arrows point in both directions because the conversation can go back and forth. The dotted lines show "short circuits," or what happens when steps are missed out. (See section i. for examples of short circuits.)

1. Choosing to communicate

The first step in the process requires that the people involved in or desiring to have a conversation choose to do so. Without a conscious choice, no conversation can take place and you might as well talk to the wall.

Choosing to communicate means *listening* (taking in the information) as well as *expressing* yourself clearly (putting out the information). When you take in data you use the five basic senses: sight, hearing, touch, smell, and taste. When you put out the information you need to be accurate and descriptive. If you beat around the bush your partner will have a difficult time understanding you. Some examples of putting out information clearly are phrases like these:

- I see you're wearing a red dress.
- I see your muscles tightening.
- I hear your voice becoming louder.

2. Understanding/assumptions/judgments

Whenever you see, hear, touch, smell, or taste something you immediately assign a meaning to it. Meanings are impressions, conclusions, assumptions, judgments, etc. All the information you take in through your senses is filtered through a screen based on past experiences and the interpretations you've put on those past experiences, as the following examples illustrate:

- I haven't seen you in that dress for awhile; *I thought you didn't like it.*
- I see you shaking; *I think you're scared.*
- I hear you shouting; *I think you're getting angry at me.*
- I can smell your new perfume; *I assume you want to make love.*

In conversation it is important to be aware of the assumptions you are making

FIGURE #6

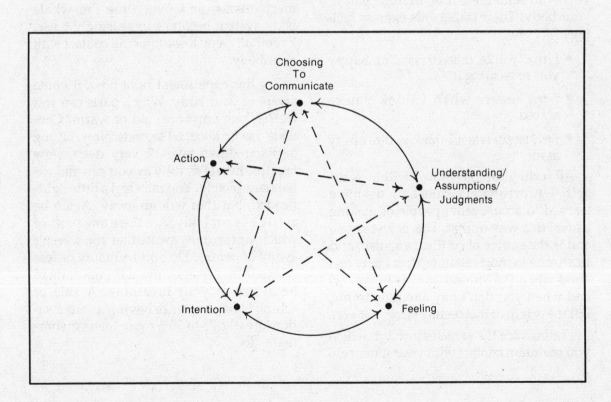

based on the information you are taking in. If you are not aware of your assumptions, you won't be able to check them out with the person you're talking to and the conversation will quickly deteriorate. For example, if you say, "Why are you wearing that dress? You don't like it," you are making a statement for her without checking it out. She will probably reply, in an annoyed tone, by saying, "I do so like it! Why? Don't you?" If, however, you make it clear that it is *your* thought, she is likely to be more willing to reply in a way that will lead to more open conversation. "I thought you didn't like that red dress." She replies, "I thought so too, but I tried it on again and liked it. I'm not sure why."

One of the basic rules of clear communication is to be aware of the assumptions you are making and to check them out with the other person.

3. Feeling

A feeling is an emotional response to the sense-oriented information you take in and the meaning you assign to it. Feeling involves an actual sensation in some part of your body. These statements express feelings:

- I really like that dress. I'm happy you're wearing it.

- *I feel uneasy* when I think you're scared.

- *I feel angry* when I think you're angry at me.

All feelings are generated within yourself. Unfortunately, most of us have learned to accuse other people of making us feel this way or that. This is just not so and is the source of conflict, anguish, and heartache in most relationships. I may feel good when I'm around you, or I may feel bad when you don't pay attention to me, but the origin of that feeling is me, not you.

Feelings are the vehicles through which you maintain contact with your inner self.

If you attribute the source of your feelings to other people, you'll lose a sense of who you are. When this happens in a relationship each person blames the other for their bad feelings which, in turn, raises the other's level of emotion. In these kinds of relationships the feelings run high but they don't make sense, and the couple will feel emotionally drained much of the time. To break the cycle of emotional reactions these couples must return to the source of their feelings (i.e., the self), and develop an awareness of their assumptions.

The more you are aware of your body, the more you will be aware of your feelings, which will help you make sense of your life because you will be aware of the assumptions you are making about the events around you. This knowledge is the key to taking charge of your life and your relationships. You can become aware of your body by monitoring your breathing. When you become tense, as in a difficult conversation, you usually hold back on your breathing. When this occurs your body cannot maintain its natural relaxation mechanisms, and over time the whole body system becomes increasingly tense. Eventually, you lose almost all contact with your body.

Try this experiment right now. Become aware of your body. Which parts can you feel? Which parts are cold or warm? Continue this for about 60 seconds. Now, sitting or lying down take 12 very deep, slow breaths. Inhale as fully as you can and exhale completely. You may feel a little light-headed, but that will go away. Again be aware of your body. Are there any parts of which you are now aware that you weren't aware of before? Do you feel more or less relaxed? In conversations it is important to be aware of your breathing. A rule of thumb is, when you're having a conversation, breathe 25 to 30% more than you normally do.

How you experience your feelings will take you in one of two directions: attraction or repulsion. If, in the presence of your partner, you are comfortable with your experienced feeling, you will want to move closer to him or her and you will relax, then experience warmth in your body. For example, Jean and Art, who were recently married, are very much in love. One afternoon Art looks at Jean in the kitchen and tells her he loves her. He gently draws her close to his body and kisses her passionately. Jean responds by feeling good about what's happening and her body heats up.

If, however, you are uncomfortable with your experienced feeling, you will draw back and feel coolness in your body. For example, Jack and Diane are in a rocky 25-year marriage. Jack, in a rare moment of spontaneity, kisses Diane on the cheek. She pulls away from him saying, "Don't!" and a coolness permeates her body.

4. Intention

In conversation it is important to be aware of intentions. The nature of each person's intentions will create the atmosphere in which the conversation is taking place. Is your intention to have a clear exchange or to clarify some misunderstanding? Is it to get to know yourself and the other better? Are you open to learning something new? These types of intentions lead to satisfying conversations. We call this goodwill, which is expressed in these examples:

- I don't understand what's happening between us right now. Would you be willing to talk with me about it?

- I have a problem. Do you have time to discuss it?

- I'm feeling awful about our fight last night. Would you be willing to talk about it?

If, however, your intention is to impose your views and opinions on the other, the exchange will likely turn sour:

- You'd better change your ways or I'm gone!

- That's not the way to do it you idiot! Here, let me show you!

- You're always spending too much money on junk like that!

5. Action

Action usually involves one person stating clearly, directly, and courteously what he or she wants. The other person responds by making a commitment to follow through on some agreed upon behavior, then doing it within a specified time period.

Dan: I want to go running with you.
Pat: I will go running with you in five minutes.

Jill: I want to make love with you.
John: I'd love to make love with you right now. Let's go to bed.

Tom: I would appreciate it if you would give me a hand.
Lee: Sure I'll give you a hand. Tell me what to do.

For many couples the action part of conversation is a missing element. You have to be willing to ask for what you want or negotiate an agreed upon course of action, then be willing to commit yourself to action and take the necessary steps to follow through. Otherwise, talking together becomes meaningless and empty because nothing ever changes as a result of your conversations.

By being aware of and following the five-step process of conversation you will be able to improve your ability to have more satisfying conversations. When the five steps are not followed or are short-circuited, confusion and misunderstandings will creep into your conversation and you will likely give up trying to talk to each other, even about the good things. Now assess your partner's communications by completing Activity #15.

i. AVOIDING SHORT CIRCUITS IN CONVERSATION

Couples commonly short-circuit their conversations by missing out important steps in the process. The dotted lines in Figure #6 show these short circuits.

1. Understanding/assumptions/ judgments ⟹ action

This short circuit is common in relationships. You hear something, think you understand, then take the action based on your assumption. It's called "assume-and-do." For example, when Frank says to Martha, "Boy, this rug is dirty," Martha assumes Frank wants it cleaned right away so she immediately pulls out the vacuum cleaner and vacuums the rug.

When you assume-and-do, you act with no awareness of your feelings or your intentions. You're likely to communicate your feelings indirectly, deny your true feelings, or appear to others to be emotionless. Men who operate on this short circuit often seem to be angry all the time while women tend to "burst into tears for no reason." These reactions are symptoms of indirect expression of feelings.

If the five steps were followed, the conversation between Frank and Martha might go like this:

Frank: "Boy this rug is dirty."

Martha: "I think you want me to vacuum it immediately, is that so?"

Frank: "No, I am amazed at how quickly it's gotten dirty. You only vacuumed it the other day."

Martha: "I feel relieved that you see these things, sometimes I feel nobody notices what I do."

Frank: "I do appreciate what you do Martha. Sometimes I feel that way too. We lead a busy life and I think we just need to learn to let some of these things go so we can have more time together. What do you think?"

Martha: "I agree. The rug can wait until next cleaning day."

2. Understanding/assumptions/ judgments ⟹ feeling ⟹ action

This short circuit happens when you don't listen to your partner. You assume you understand what the other is saying, experience a feeling, then act on that feeling. The result is that your actions are not in response to the reality of the other person. Your behavior does not make sense to your partner, although it may to you. You may be accused of being pushy, abusive, unloving, or selfish.

EXAMPLE

Joe is divorced and is now in a relationship with Dawn. He has four older children plus three grandchildren. Joe and his ex-wife are now friends and talk on the phone every couple of weeks. He also loves his children very much and likes to visit them to see his grandchildren. Joe has made it clear to Dawn that he loves her and wants to be with her only. He has also explained to Dawn that he and his ex-wife have a long history together and that because she sometimes has difficulties he is not about to completely abandon her. But whenever Joe talks to his ex-wife, Dawn flies off the handle and tells him to never talk to with his ex again. She says that if Joe really loved her he wouldn't talk to his ex-wife. Dawn's difficulty is that she doesn't really listen to Joe and in her own insecurity is afraid that Joe will return to his ex-wife. Dawn must listen closely to Joe and trust his words, intentions, and actions if her communications around this issue are ever going to be settled.

COMMUNICATION ASSESSMENT OF YOUR PARTNER

How communicative is your partner?

Answer each statement by writing in the number that best describes your partner.

1. Never true
2. Hardly ever
3. Sometimes
4. Almost always true
5. Always true

_____ My partner likes talking with me one-to-one when no one else is around.

_____ My partner includes me in small group conversations.

_____ My partner includes himself or herself in conversations with friends.

_____ My partner willingly talks with me about our conflicts.

_____ I find my partner easy to talk with.

_____ My partner tells me when something is bothering him or her.

_____ My partner tells me when and how she or he appreciates me.

_____ My partner listens to me.

_____ I think I understand my partner's inner life.

_____ I think my partner communicates well with me.

_____ My partner can get his or her ideas across to me clearly and simply.

_____ TOTAL

The higher you've scored your partner (out of a total of 55), the better you feel about his or her willingness to communicate with you. If the score is less than 30, in your view your partner is uncommunicative. You are likely to feel resentment toward him or her.

3. Confusing understanding/ assumptions/judgments with feelings

The confusion between a thought and a feeling is a very common difficulty in communications between couples. Not only is it inaccurate, but it leads to messy, confused exchanges. It can also be an attempt to manipulate the other by putting the power of a feeling behind the statement. For example, "I feel you should be more honest," stated directly would be, "I think you're lying to me; I want you to tell me the truth." Or, "I feel you should read this chapter on communications," stated more accurately is "I'm learning some things that I believe would help our communications; I think you could learn something by reading this chapter too. I think we both need some help in this area."

Often, the statement "I feel you..." is an indirect way of stating a judgment. It is more honest to declare your judgments. Also, the other person can respond more easily and directly to a clear judgment than to some amorphous feeling.

4. Taking in ➡ feeling „ action

This short circuit means you act without thinking. Your actions are really emotional reactions. You don't think about what assumptions you're making about information you're taking in, nor do you think about what you are trying to achieve with your actions. This short circuit can lead to explosive kinds of behavior that result in verbal or physical confrontations. For example, after Fred and Joyce have been bickering for about five minutes, Joyce, in frustration, finally says, "You're just like your father — always pushing people around." Fred takes it in, feels threatened by it, and yells at Joyce, "Oh yeah, you're just like that cold bitch mother of yours!" In order to break the cycle these two have to slow down their exchange, examine their assumptions and stop to think about what their intentions are. It will likely take

an outside referee because this kind of short circuit is so highly charged.

5. Understanding/assumption/ judgment ➡ feeling

This short circuit involves no overt action. In essence, the person displays a feeling but then withdraws inside. Usually the individual's responses are reactions to the people around him or her and therefore the individual will feel controlled by them or, to put it another way, will feel impotent or victimized by his or her partner. The person makes assumptions based on what is said or done, then experiences a feeling based on that assumption but is not aware of what might be the appropriate action in the situation. For example, Sean, upon seeing Sara burning the dinner exclaims, "What are you doing?" Sara bursts into tears and runs into the bathroom. Or, when Don is trying to fix the stove for the tenth time, Jean walks in and asks, "What are you doing that for?" Don, without saying a word, slams down the screwdriver and stomps off in a huff. This short circuit is a sign that the individuals feel powerless to act. They must begin to examine their assumptions about their personal worth, take a look at what they want to achieve, then take the necessary action to make that happen.

6. Intention ➡ action

This short circuit represents behavior you engage in when you don't take in information from the other. You are also not interested in examining your assumptions or judgments and you are not aware of feeling anything. Your sole intention is to get what you want, which is indicative of the stance in the power struggle stage: *It's my way or the highway!*

Your intention is to manipulate the other person or control his or her behavior so you can achieve your ends. Your actions are cold and calculated. At these times people can deal with you only by choosing not to engage in your manipulations and by cutting off any contact with you until you are willing to listen to another's point of view and risk exploring your true feelings.

With this information about the dynamics of conversation in mind, evaluate the conversations between you and your partner in Activity #16.

ACTIVITY #16
EVALUATING YOUR CONVERSATIONS

Think about three important conversations you've had with your partner in the last two weeks. Write down the main topic you were discussing.

1. _____

2. _____

3. _____

For each conversation, answer the following questions:

1. Did it_____go well? _____get short circuited?

2. Take a look at Figure #6. Which of the following steps in the process of conversation were included:

_____ (a) Choosing to communicate

_____ (b) Understanding/assumptions/judgments

_____ (c) Feeling

_____ (d) Intention

_____ (e) Action

3. At which step was the conversation short-circuited? _____

_____

4. Who short-circuited this conversation?_____

_____

Once you have answered the questions for all three conversations, decide whether you can see a pattern. Are your conversations being short-circuited at the same stage each time? or by the same person each time? What could you do to change the pattern?

_____

_____

_____

_____

Have a conversation with your partner in which each of you follows the five steps.

_____

_____

_____

_____

_____

6

WHAT'S THERE TO TALK ABOUT ANYWAY?

There are many reasons why people become involved in intimate relationships, but there are only four fundamental issues over which couples fight or terminate their relationships. They are love, sex, money, and sex roles.

a. LOVE

Philosophers, scholars, theologians, gurus, and psychologists have been trying to define love since time immemorial. But their efforts, while interesting, have only some relevance to your relationship because the experience of love is personal. There may be universal guiding principles that must be followed in order to create an environment in which love can be experienced, but *you* determine whether or not love can exist and how it needs to be expressed so that you can experience it.

These are the main considerations in an intimate relationship:

(a) Can I really allow myself to be loved? What blocks do I put up to stop myself from experiencing your love?

(b) In this relationship, what does my partner do that tells me he or she loves me? Do these behaviors help me to become a more authentic, healthy individual? Or do they interfere with my sense of being a person?

(c) What are the things that I do as a way of trying to express my love for my partner? Are these the ways in which my partner wants to be loved? Do they serve to smother her or him, or

do they help my partner become a more unique, healthy individual?

(d) How can we help each other experience more love?

The answers to these questions are found in your attitudes toward loving and being loved, and the source of those attitudes is found in your personal history. Why are you attracted to particular kinds of men or women? And what is the fascination beneath the initial attractions?

Dr. Carl Jung, the world famous psychoanalyst and a contemporary of Sigmund Freud, argued that every man has a feminine side to his being, which is his *anima*, and every woman has a masculine side to her, called her *animus*. As part of the socialization process, a male, while learning to become a man as society defines it (i.e., never cry, be tough, sacrifice self for career, etc.), represses his feminine self and is repulsed by the idea that he might have feminine qualities. A female undergoes the same kind of socialization process and loses touch with her masculine self, which would be outgoing, rational, hard, assertive, directed, and goal oriented. This doesn't mean that she doesn't possess these qualities, but that she is not aware of them in herself and will go to great lengths to deny them and hide them. Men, of course, also take great pains to hide or deny that part of themselves that is romantic, nurturing, soft, passive, and receptive. According to Jung, when a man falls in love with a woman he is really falling in love with those feminine aspects of himself of which he is unaware. The same applies to a woman who falls in love. She is attracted to those masculine qualities that she does not see in herself but only sees in her lover.

Since our parents, or people who replaced our parents, play a large part in socializing us to become men and women, we, in a strange twist of unconscious logic, choose intimates who have our parents' traits. The reason we do this is to try to find a replacement for our lost animus or anima — the other half of ourselves. We think our partner will make us feel good because he or she has the qualities that we gave up in the process of becoming a woman or man. Unfortunately, when we choose a partner who is like our parents we also pick the kind of person who is most difficult for us to love because we're still angry at our parents for making us give up an important part of ourselves. This happens when we're told, "Don't be a sissy; big boys don't cry," or, "Don't do that, it's not ladylike," or, "Look at you, clinging to your mother's apron strings."

We inevitably shift that anger onto our present partners. We also make it very difficult for our partners to love us because often the things they do remind us, unconsciously, of the pain we experienced in childhood. In reaction to that unconscious reminder we punish our partner for childhood hurts. As a result, our present relationships become hurtful and full of conflict but we don't understand why it is happening.

The way to overcome these difficulties is to figure out why we pick our intimates. When we become aware of our patterns of selection, we can then take the steps to learn how to love and be loved. For this process to be most effective, both you and your partner must be willing to complete the following activities. You can, however, learn a lot about yourself by doing it alone, then talking with a trusted friend about what you've learned.

1. Your parental profile

Activity #17 will help you develop a profile of each of your parents (or significant adults in your life) as a first step toward establishing your particular pattern of selection in choosing a partner.

You now have a picture of all the positive and negative traits you unconsciously look for when you are looking for a lover. When you met with your partner your heart skipped a beat and you had that uncanny feeling that you'd known him or her all your life. In a way, you were right because your partner represents the unconscious you. You fell in love with him or her because of many familiar positive traits. But to make the relationship really interesting, he or she also had to have negative aspects, just like your parents. Without knowing it, you tuned in to these negative things. But, being swept up in your romantic fantasies (love is blind to the negative), you only saw your partner's positive qualities. The elixir of romance blinded you to the negative aspects in your lover and led you to believe that your unconscious dream had finally come true: you had, at last, found your Prince or Princess Charming — the person who would give you all the love and attention you didn't get as a child.

But alas, the dream is just that. In the cold light of day it becomes painfully evident that your partner is a person with all the same shortcomings your parents had. There is, however, one big difference: because you are both equal adults you can agree to acknowledge your desire for the illusion to be true and enter the world of mature relationships. Talk with your partner about your findings. Take responsibility for your part in the creation of the romantic illusion. Take the risk of being yourselves while being together. Discuss how each of you wants the other to live out your anima or animus for you. For example, if a man, do you let your partner do

ACTIVITY #17
RECOLLECTIONS OF MOMMY AND DADDY

1. Write 10 words or phrases that you would use to describe your mother as you remember her from your childhood. (Some examples are the words kind, happy, she hugged me a lot, angry, religious, always there when I needed her. It's all right if your list contains contradictions. People do have contradictory personality traits; an angry mother can still be kind.)

1. _____
2. _____
3. _____
4. _____
5. _____
6. _____
7. _____
8. _____
9. _____
10. _____

2. Write 10 words or phrases that you would use to describe your father.

1. _____
2. _____
3. _____
4. _____
5. _____
6. _____
7. _____
8. _____
9. _____
10. _____

3. If there was another significant adult in your childhood, write 10 words or phrases that you would use to describe her or him.

1. _____
2. _____
3. _____
4. _____
5. _____

6. _____

7. _____

8. _____

9. _____

10. _____

4. Go through each list and put a plus sign (+) beside each description you judge to be positive, and a minus sign (-) beside each description you remember as negative.

5. Draw a large circle in the space below. Divide it in half, vertically. On the left side of the circle write all the negative descriptions of both your parents and/or significant adult. Put all the positive descriptions on the right side.

most of the nurturing? If a woman, do you want your partner to be the gentle aggressor (i.e., your knight in shining armor)? What effect does that have on your relationship?

2. Your childhood profile

Now let's take a look at your experience of being a child. Activity #18 will help you articulate your buried desires and needs that you are still carrying from childhood.

You are likely still seeking to fulfill these desires in your relationships today. It is also probable that you try to fulfill these desires in indirect ways, then blame your partner for not being sensitive to your needs. For example, if you wanted recognition from your father, but didn't get it, you may react by being ambitious in your career to the point of ignoring your partner. When you want to relax with your partner, but he or she is indifferent because of your absence over the past few months, you may accuse your partner of being unappreciative of the hard work that you do "so you can both have a good home." In this case, your workaholism is an unconscious attempt to show your father how good you really are so that he will finally pay attention to you.

The activities in the following sections will help you to be more direct and more aware of the kind of partner you have chosen.

3. Your partner profile

Activity #19 (like the one you did for your parents) will help you develop a profile of your partner as you see and experience his or her behavior.

4. Your behavior profile in relationship

Activity #20 explores your frustrations with your partner and your way of reacting to those frustrations, as a means of finding out what you really want in your relationship.

When we're frustrated or hurt we usually try to find some way to punish our partner in an attempt to get our partner to do what we want. Sherry goes silent and sulks when she thinks Cecil isn't spending enough time with her. Cecil stops being kind and affectionate when he thinks Sherry is not interested enough in sex.

But why would Cecil want to spend time with Sherry when she is sulking? By the same token Sherry is not going to be interested in having sex with Cecil if he's not being kind and affectionate. They have to change their behaviors if they ever hope to break the stalemate and experience more love. Before they can do that they must be aware of what each wants.

5. A return to loving and being loved

A lover is a person who can, with charm and integrity, find out what another wants and be willing to give it in a loving manner. This is relatively easy at the romantic stage of a relationship because each of you will do anything to please and is pleased by practically anything your lover does. However, as the romance fades and you become more used to one another it is necessary to put a deliberate effort into renewing and revitalizing your love. Romantic love is spontaneous; deepening mature love evolves through the art of conversation. Activity #21 will help you do that.

Over time, as you begin to experience more love together, each of you will feel you want to give more and receive more. Each of you will then be more in touch with your animus or anima, which means you will feel free to be yourself in a relationship because you won't be frustrated by encumbrances from your childhood.

ACTIVITY #18
EXPLORING YOUR CHILDHOOD DESIRES

1. Write a list of the ways in which your mother and father let you down when you were a child — things that you wanted from them but didn't get (e.g., my mother never let me alone; my father never praised my efforts).

_____

_____

_____

_____

_____

_____

_____

_____

_____

2. Write a list of the things you got but didn't want (e.g., my dad hit me; my mother yelled at me).

_____

_____

_____

_____

_____

_____

_____

_____

These lists represent your childhood frustrations; behind each of your frustrations is an unfulfilled desire.

3. Look at your lists. Rewrite each item as a desire. For example, beside "my father never praised me" you might write, "I wish my father would praise me."

_____

_____

_____

_____

_____

_____

_____

_____

_____

4. Now write each desire as if you were speaking directly to your mother or father. Write exactly what it is that you want. For example, write, "Dad, I wish you would praise me and let me know how proud you are of me when I do well and come home excited to tell you about it," or, "Mom, instead of yelling at me I wish you would listen to me and understand how hard it is for me to do what you want as quickly as you want it. Please have some patience with me."

_____

_____

_____

_____

_____

_____

_____

_____

_____

5. Examine your list of desires. If you could be a child again and your mother was willing to fulfill any desire if you asked, which would it be? Circle that desire. What feelings come to you as you consider this possibility?

6. If your father was willing to fulfill one desire if you asked, which would it be? Circle that desire. What feelings are you aware of as you think about this?

7. Have a conversation with your partner about what you're learning.

ACTIVITY #19
PROFILING YOUR PARTNER

1. Write 10 words or phrases that you would use to describe your partner. Put a plus sign (+) next to each description that you judge to be positive and a minus sign (-) beside each that you judge to be negative.

1. _____
2. _____
3. _____
4. _____
5. _____
6. _____
7. _____
8. _____
9. _____
10. _____

2. On the left side of the circle below, write all the negative descriptions and on the right all the positive descriptions.

3. Compare this profile with that of your parents to see how closely the two match up. If they don't match up very much and your present relationship is not very satisfying, you may find it useful to go over the above activities again to see if you've left out some critical information.

4. Talk with your partner about the profile you drew of him or her. Remember these are your judgments based on the information you've taken in about your partner. Your partner may not see it the same way. Discuss the similarities and differences.

1. Take a piece of paper and fold it in half, lengthwise. On the left side of the fold write seven frustrations that you have with your partner — the kinds of behavior that you want but don't get, plus behavior you get but don't want. Be specific. For example, Sherry might write, "I'm frustrated that you never spend enough time with me," or Cecil might write, "I'm frustrated because you're only interested in having sex once a month." Leave plenty of space between each item on your list.

2. On the right side of the folded paper, write three things next to each frustration: first, how you feel about the frustration (e.g., "angry and hurt"); second, what you do in response (e.g., "withdraw"); third, your intention behind your action (e.g., "to get as far away from you as possible").

3. Refer back to your "frustration list." Restate each frustration as a desire. Be specific. For example, Sherry might write, "I want us to spend at least two evenings a week alone together, talking or just engaging in some kind of relaxation that we both enjoy." Cecil might say, "I want you to be more responsive to me sexually."

When you and your partner have each finished these three steps, spend some time talking together about your lists.

ACTIVITY #21
GETTING WHAT YOU DESIRE

You and your partner should each complete the following lists.

1. Complete the following statement in as many ways as you are able.
Currently, I feel cared about and loved when you

_____

_____

_____

_____

_____

_____

2. Think about those things that you want your partner to do, but are afraid to ask for. Use the following statement: *I would feel cared about and loved if you would be willing to*

_____

_____

_____

_____

3. For each of the above responses, write down the ways in which you interfere or might interfere with your partner caring for and loving you.

_____

_____

_____

_____

4. Go over your responses and rank them in order of importance to you.

5. Talk with your partner about your lists. Put an X beside those items that your partner is unwilling to do for you.

b. SEX

The following lyrics from the song "Sexual Intelligence"* by Parachute Club clearly express the difficulties and challenges facing men and women in relationships today.

He learned the rules as a normal boy
She learned them too
  but they weren't quite the same
He learned how to fight.
He learned how to win.
She learned how to smile, and to stand
  there by him
They called it common sense
They grew up so different
They were the typical children
Livin' in a myth!

We're gonna dream of when
In friendship we walk hand in hand
To know each other well
We look to find intelligence.

As they grew up, they would realize
They learned it too young.
They had learned it too well
Now wearing costumes of man & wife
Resenting each other and not knowing
  why
They couldn't see the sense
They were caught up in the difference
They were typical lovers
Watching love's goodbye.

...The world that they lived in
Had turned them both around
The fear they felt inside

...Facing each other's pain
Choosing to try again
Talking about new values
Building up confidence

Sexual intelligence
On the way to self-respect
They were just typical people

No longer in a myth
We're gonna dream of when

In friendship we walk hand in hand
To know each other well
We seek to find
Intelligence!
Sexual Intelligence!

The song shows that we have to develop our intelligence in regard to heterosexual relationships. The myths, dreams, assumptions, judgments, phobias, and just plain "dumb" ideas we carry into our sexual encounters lead to life-long resentments, pain, and misunderstandings. The most effective way of overcoming those misunderstandings is through the art of conversation. Chapter 8, "Sex in Long-Term Relationships," will present some ideas about how to overcome misunderstandings and some methods for you to try.

c. MONEY

If sex is the reason that people get together, money is usually the thing that couples fight about the most and that causes them to eventually separate. The battle over money seems to lead to irreconcilable differences that continue into the divorce courts. But conflicts over money — who earns it, controls it, or spends it — are really about the more basic issues of freedom and responsibility.

Freedom and *responsibility*, like the proverbial horse and carriage, always go together. The degree of freedom that you experience in your life is directly proportional to the amount of responsibility you are willing to take for the decisions you make in life. It follows then, that if you are not experiencing your freedom, you are not taking responsibility for your decisions.

EXAMPLE

George married Sara 10 years ago but now feels hemmed in by her and the children. He doesn't tell her this directly but criticizes

---

*By permission of the songwriters, Lorraine Segato, Billy Bryans, Lauri Conger, Lynne Fernie, and Dave Gray, and by the publisher, Current Sounds, a Division of The Current Entertainment Corporation, Toronto, Canada.

her for mishandling the family finances and is resentful that "kids cost so much to bring up these days." But in fact, George is not willing to make the choice either to leave his family or deal with the consequences of the choices he had made 10 years ago and stay and be happy with Sara and the children. His freedom is not in his family's hands, it is in his willingness to make a decision and to responsibly follow through on it. Sara, in return, occasionally messes up her budget or splurges on items that she knows will infuriate George. Her splurges are indirect ways of showing George, and herself, that she is free. Her budgetary mismanagement is her unwillingness to take responsibility for the fact that she chooses to stay in an unloving relationship. They have been fighting about these things for the last seven years.

Many people have never made a real decision. Most people "go with the flow" and experience themselves as victims of fate, or other people. Only when the absence of choice leads to painful symptoms and extreme unhappiness do they feel an urgency to take a serious look at what a decision really is. Most people attempt to make the "right" decision; but to look for what is "right" and "correct" in a decision is to avoid making a decision. Would it be right for George to go or stay? Neither decision is right; either has serious long-term consequences.

The most important problems in relationships are insoluble because there is no one "right" answer. Choices are real only when "right" answers either do not exist or are irrelevant. In making those kinds of choices we become aware of the depth of personal responsibility and the anxiety of freedom. Many people would rather not decide than experience that anxiety. George badgers Sara about the money rather than face his options. Sara mismanages the money knowing that George will criticize her and that she will feel victimized, which is better than trying to make it alone with two children. Both are miserable.

When a couple gets married or moves in together they are giving up a large chunk of their freedom for the security of always having another person around. This is not meant as a cynical statement but simply as one of the many consequences of these kinds of decisions. Most of us are reluctant to allow ourselves to experience the anxiety of what it means to risk making an authentic decision. It would be useful to keep these things in mind when you argue about money.

EXAMPLES

1. Cathy and Merle were married recently. They both work. In the last few months Merle has been criticizing Cathy for spending too much money on clothes. In fact, Cathy has cut back her spending since their marriage because she is aware of the added expenses. When they fight about it Cathy thinks Merle is treating her like a child and she becomes angry. The issue at hand here is how much freedom can Merle tolerate from his wife? He is facing his anxiety about having made the choice to marry a woman who is independent in her thinking, which is very powerfully symbolized in her earning an independent income. In this power struggle Cathy will have to make it clear to Merle that in order for the relationship to work for her, Merle will have to respect her freedom and her decision-making abilities. If there is a problem she wants him to talk about it, not criticize her.

2. Sue and John are in their early 50s and have been married for 25 years. Sue is becoming anxious because she doesn't know their financial details. John has always given her an allowance each month for running the house. He has looked after everything else. He often complains about money but is never specific; he just makes vague statements like, "I don't know how I'm going to be able to make ends meet!" Sue wants John to tell her about their financial picture. He resists, saying, "Don't worry, everything's fine, I've taken care of things for the last 25 years and it's worked out." Sue is angry but the more she persists, the more he resists.

Sue, in wanting to know about the finances, is demanding a major change in their relationship. She willingly gave up a lot of personal freedom to marry John and to raise their children. She has no regrets about that. John also gave up some of his freedom to hold down a steady job and be responsible for their money. But Sue now wants more freedom from the role of wife and mother. Her children are grown up and she sees how other women are finding new meaning in their lives separate from their husbands and families. She doesn't want to leave John; she wants to renegotiate their relationship. And while John has had the responsibility for money matters he has also experienced the freedom to do what he likes with it, without someone else questioning his decisions. The money issue can be the vehicle for John and Sara to renegotiate their freedoms and responsibilities. It will require long, intense conversations before a successful outcome is reached.

Self-pity and blame are two common stances that couples take in their fights over money. But self-pity and blame, the conviction that you feel victimized by life or by your partner, are symptoms that you are denying your freedom as well as the awareness that you can make other choices. A shortage of money limits your choices in the material world but it does not limit your subjective freedom or your ability to be happy. (This assumes that your basic needs have been met for food, shelter, clothing, and safety.) Some of the richest people in the world are miserable.

Of all the topics that couples fight over, money is the one that will test your communication skills to the limits. The following activity will help you to talk more openly and rationally about your money problems.

If you choose to be in a relationship, you must be willing to take responsibility for the fact that you are also limiting your freedom to some degree. It's no different than choosing one item from a menu and in doing so giving up the freedom to taste the rest of the dishes.

You are free to choose what you do and whatever you want with your money when you are single. But when with another, your decisions have an impact on him or her, and mature love demands that you seriously consider your partner. This means talking with your partner with the intention of making a decision that is an expression of love from both of you.

When you take responsibility for this, you also experience your freedom; in so doing, you will be happy no matter what the decision.

ACTIVITY #22
EXAMINING YOUR ATTITUDES TO MONEY

With your partner take turns completing the following statements:

To me money is _____

_____

As a child, money was _____

_____

My father's attitude toward money was _____

_____

My mother's attitude toward money was _____

_____

With regard to our finances, I'm most afraid that _____

_____

One of the ways I try to control the way you spend money is _____

_____

I think I handle money _____

One thing that I need to learn about money is _____

_____

Right now I feel _____

I would like you to _____

I get angry about how you spend money when _____

I limit my spending by _____

I deny myself (name three things)

1. _____

2. _____

3. _____

_____ ... because I think we can't afford them.

When I deny myself, I feel _____

I think you criticize me unfairly for _____

_____

In regard to money, I think you don't understand _____

_____

One of the ways I spite you is _____

_____

Concerning our financial affairs, right now I'm aware that _____

I sometimes spend money frivolously because _____

I get tight with money when_____

It's easier for me to criticize you about how you spend money than it is to _____

_____

If I didn't worry about money I'd be free to_____

When I want to indulge myself I buy _____

In regard to money I blame you for_____

If I didn't blame you, I'd have to face the fact that _____

In regard to money I would like you to (name three things you want your partner to change)

1. _____

2. _____

3. _____

I hate myself most when _____

In regard to money I need to change (name three behaviors you are willing to change)

1. _____

2. _____

3. _____

One of the ways I try to control how you spend money is _____

I leave decisions about money to you in the following areas _____

_____

Three major mistakes about money management I've made in the last seven years are

1. _____

2. _____

3. _____

I think I will have "arrived" when I have _____... dollars in the bank.

In regard to our finances, I would like you to let me know when I _____

_____

In regard to money, I hope that we can_____

_____

_____

_____

d. SEX ROLES

Up until 25 years ago an uneasy equilibrium, dating back to the beginnings of the Industrial Revolution, existed between men and women. The Industrial Revolution, with its demand for factory workers, meant that the concept of family had to be completely redefined. The workplace was separated from the home which resulted in the separation of men's work and women's work. Men's work was valued over women's work because men earned the money. Women's work was intended to support the outside activities of the man. This separation of sex roles led to cooperation between the sexes by avoidance: i.e., Mary washes the dishes while John fixes the car; Mary does the laundry while John cuts the grass, and never the twain shall meet. Love was also separated from work because of the split between home and the workplace. Fathers became alienated from their children since the work demands of a 60- to 100-hour work week left little energy to deal with the responsibilities of parenthood. Children were often told they shouldn't "bother father," because he had to save his energy to go to work. This is how children came to fear and/or idolize this mostly absent, rather mysterious figure. Children often had contact with their father only when he was lecturing, punishing, or abusing them. It is easy to understand how, within this environment, sex roles became so rigid.

Five major phenomena have occurred within the last 25 years that have created a revolution in male/female/family relationships. First, the women's movement illuminated unthought of possibilities for women in all spheres. Second, the entry of women into the work force began the move toward economic independence for many women, and with it the responsibility of making the choice of who will raise the children. Third, the widespread use of the pill on one hand put the decision about whether or not to have a child into the woman's control, while on the other hand raised the painful dilemma of how she defined herself as a woman. Fourth, the movement toward convicting spouse batterers and child abusers changed women's perspective about men being the stronger sex and made it obvious how quickly men, when they feel powerless, will resort to violence (verbal or physical) rather than admit their vulnerability. Fifth, the increasing outrage over the pain and death caused by drunk drivers (who are mostly men) has changed society's attitude that a man should be allowed his "indulgences" for sacrificing himself in the working world. Men are being called upon to take more responsibility for all their actions when it affects the people they are supposed to care for and love.

The last two phenomena represent a demand by society for men to "grow up." On the surface, men appear to have much to lose: they will have to compete with women for jobs and promotion; they will have to give up some behaviors that are part of their learned definition of what it means to be a man and learn behaviors that are seen as "feminine" and are much less valued in this society (e.g., being nurturing and supportive at home); they will have to give up some control in order to win intimacy. It's relatively easy to get someone at work to do something for you if you're in control and you can use coercion if necessary, but at home where you want a more equal, loving relationship, negotiation with goodwill and compassion will more likely get you what you want. Control is the antithesis of intimacy. Men will have to be more willing to face their weaknesses and give up their obsession with domination. It is against this cultural backdrop that men and women will have to work out their relationships.

Dual career couples are in the forefront of creating new rules for sex roles in relationships with only a tentative idea of what the new values and appropriate roles will be. The current crop of two-paycheck couples is a generation in transition. Most of us grew up in a world of the traditional family and have been flung into a world in which the rules have been changed, but the players have not been notified.

If sociological events were the only source of sex-role problems, it would be a simple matter for men and women to re-educate themselves. But the conflict and anger that is generated between women and men in the battle for equality goes much deeper. The roots of the divisions lie in the developmental psychology of men and women. A very brief outline of those dynamics is presented here.

1. How boys become men

In order to become "men," boys in our society have to relinquish identification with their mothers. This happens at several significant times in a boy's life: at age 5 to 6 when he begins play school; at 7 to 8 years when he starts school full time; at puberty; when he first experiences "puppy love"; when he starts dating and becomes sexually active (whether the activity is real or fantasized); when he leaves home for the first time; when he enters the work world; when he gets married or becomes intimately involved with a woman. During these events a male experiences a profound upheaval in his internal psychic life because he is leaving the nurturing, predictable, albeit controlling, environment that his mother provides. As a result, he feels completely vulnerable and helpless. It is during these times that his father should be playing the role of nurturer and guide to the external, often unfriendly, world. But because most fathers are not available to their sons, boys develop defenses to protect themselves from the fear and pain they experience.

Boys/men become independent, aggressive, strong, and insular. In later life it is difficult for them to be nurturing, feeling, and vulnerable, which are the qualities needed for intimate relationships. Although many men seem content and successful with these limitations, they are emotionally impoverished because of their insulation from others. Thus, when men do hunger for the comforting intimacy they experienced as a child, they turn to women. But because of the deep sense of betrayal they feel toward women, they only open up as much as necessary to achieve the good feelings of being close. In times of conflict they shut off and return to their safe isolation. The sense of betrayal by father is much more profound and so men do not allow themselves to become intimate at all with each other unless they are drunk or intoxicated some other way. In a nutshell, men are even less vulnerable with other men than they are with women.

The "weak male ego" is also created in the absence of father. Being exposed to a rather unfriendly world is a fearful event that most children can't handle alone. A boy needs a male person who will guide him through the fearful times, protect him from too much anxiety, encourage him when he fails, and acknowledge and allow him to have his feelings. Without this wise guidance a boy steels himself for the onslaught. He maintains an image of "having it all together" on the outside, while feeling incompetent and weak on the inside — at least in the realm of intimate relationships. He seeks out women for the nurture he doesn't know how to give himself and won't get from other men. But his openness to being nurtured is contingent on the woman being agreeable and passive. Any resistance on her part brings back his defenses.

There are two ways out for a man. First, he can make the courageous decision to face the truth of his dilemma and risk engaging in an intimate relationship with a woman. This means facing his fears and the feelings of weakness he experiences as he

ARE YOU HOLDING UP YOUR END OF THE HOUSEWORK?

It is sad but true that in most cases men who are in two-paycheck relationships do not take equal responsibility when it comes to housework. Nothing will kill a woman's passion in the bedroom more than the thought that "he leaves it all up to me!" The following quiz is designed to help men assess how well they are sharing household responsibilities.

Rate yourself for each item. Then add up all the numbers for a total score.

0 — Never do this

1 — Occasionally I do this without being asked

2 — I voluntarily do my fair share of this

3 — Most of the time without being asked

4 — Always, when needed

BEDROOM

_____ I make the bed if I'm last out

_____ I make the children's/guest's bed

_____ I pick up my clothes

_____ I change and wash the linen

BATHROOM

_____ I clean up after I shower/bath

_____ I empty out the wastebasket

_____ I sit down when I urinate

_____ I clean up the sink after myself

_____ I clean the toilet

CLEANING

_____ I clear out old newspapers, magazine, junk mail

_____ I put my shoes, coat, etc. away

_____ I straighten up the house when needed

_____ I dust, vacuum, sweep the floor regularly

_____ I clean up after myself after working on a project

KITCHEN

_____ I regularly clean up the kitchen

_____ I help plan the meals

_____ I shop for groceries and put them away

_____ I keep track of when we are running out of things and replace them

_____ I set and clear the table

_____ I help with party preparations and clean-up

_____ I periodically clean out/defrost the fridge

_____ I share in cooking meals

_____ I clean up after myself

LAUNDRY

_____ I launder clothes when needed

_____ I fold the laundry and put it away

_____ I iron my own clothes

_____ I sew on buttons

_____ I do the children's laundry

_____ I clean the lint catcher in the dryer

_____ I buy soap when necessary

CHILDREN

_____ I make uninterrupted, non-structured time for them, at least 1 hour a day

_____ I help out with school work

_____ I help them get ready for school

_____ I change diapers and help with potty

_____ I get up at night if they are afraid or sick

_____ I make meals for them

_____ I bath them

_____ I help them dress or find their lost clothing

_____ I make arrangements for "babysitting"

_____ I put them to bed

_____ I take them to various appointments

_____ They come to me for their emotional needs and wants

_____ My partner feels I can take care of them just as well as she does

MAINTENANCE AND REPAIRS

_____ I do the "fix-up" projects around the house

_____ I buy the parts needed for household repairs

_____ I replace lightbulbs, fuses, broken windows

_____ I catch insects and rodents

GARBAGE

_____ I take it out

_____ I sort the recyclables

_____ I put it out and take it in on garbage days

OUTSIDE

_____ I cut the grass

_____ I do the watering

_____ I rake the leaves

_____ I maintain the gardens

_____ I shovel, hose the walks

VEHICLES

_____ I keep it/them clean, inside and out

_____ I arrange for repairs

_____ I keep track of the regular maintenance

_____ I gas up the car when necessary

PERSONAL

_____ I write my own mother and other family members

_____ I run my own errands

_____ I pack my own bags for trips

_____ I make my own dental, medical, etc. appointments

Talk with your partner about your self-ratings. Does she agree with you? Are you both satisfied with your (and her) participation in the household chores? All those tasks may be too much for even both of you to handle. If both of you are feeling burdened by the enormity of the household chores, consider hiring a house cleaner to come in every two weeks so you have time to relax. It will improve your sex life. If you need to negotiate household responsibilities, think about:

(a) What do you want more of?

(b) What do you want less of?

(c) What's just right?

gets close to women. Or, he can find a man or group of men to work with who are able and willing to explore the male dilemma together and to finish the task of becoming a person who knows himself as a male, a man, and as an individual. Both ways require that he take the risk of being vulnerable and ask for help. He cannot do it on his own.

2. The woman's sex role

Women have their own difficult task in their relationships with men. Generally, because of women's development, they have learned how to have friendships with each other. These friendships rest on shared intimacies, self-disclosure, nurture, and emotional support. In a relationship with a man who is willing to risk intimacy, a woman must risk being herself and exposing her toughness, harshness, and judgments she has about men. She is not all sweetness and light as she might lead him to believe. She too, has her hidden agendas for the relationship. The sex roles she learned may work in relationship with other women but she too, because of the absence of or domination by her father, has a defensive passiveness. *In order for this change to occur, her partner must be willing to* *explore it with her first.* The initial development and growth of many male/female relationships depends on *his* willingness to engage. You can't get in the house until the door is opened and you're invited in.

The conflicts and power struggles over sex-role issues like washing the dishes, equal care of the children, putting the clothes in the hamper, and grocery shopping serve as vehicles to clear up the dilemmas outlined above. Without knowledge of these things, a willingness to explore the source of one's attitudes about sex roles, developing the communications skills for working through these issues, and the desire to risk new behaviors, the battle over sex roles will go in circles. Two-career couples will have to discipline themselves to spend time making the adjustments, working out compromises, learning from the inevitable mistakes that new experiences bring and making difficult choices about their priorities. Only through open dialogue can men and women discover what's important to each other and how to reach an equitable balance of work and love. In the next chapter, "Dealing with Conflict and Anger," you will have an opportunity to continue that process.

ACTIVITY #24
EXPLORING ALTERNATIVE ROLES

Write down all your sex roles (mother, father, wife, husband, provider, nurturer, etc.)

_____

_____

_____

_____

Which do you feel burdened by?

_____

_____

_____

Which are a pleasure to you?

_____

_____

_____

Think of yourself without your sex roles. What would your life be like if you could abandon some of them?

_____

_____

Switch roles with your partner for a day. Do everything he or she would do and vice versa. Then answer the following questions.

Which of your partner's roles are most difficult for you?

_____

_____

Why? _____

_____

Which of your roles are the most difficult for you to give up?

_____

_____

Why?_____

_____

7
DEALING WITH CONFLICT AND ANGER

Your ability to create love and intimacy is directly proportional to your skills and willingness to deal effectively with conflict and anger. It's easy to love and feel close when things are going well, but your mutual respect and goodwill is tested in times of antagonism or disagreement. Conflicts, power struggles, anger, or frustrations are the inevitable by-products of intimate relationships because the closer you get to your partner, the more your different individual needs and values become apparent. Unfortunately, this reality runs counter to the romantic belief that the more you love each other, the more you will think and feel alike. Compounding this mistaken assumption is the fact that most of us have not learned how to deal effectively with conflict and anger, which is a major factor contributing to the amount of strife in all interpersonal relationships today.

a. STRATEGIES FOR RESOLVING CONFLICT

The ability and willingness to resolve conflict successfully is one of the most important social skills you can possess. This skill alone will help you gain self-confidence and the respect of people around you.

As children each of us developed reactions to conflict that were intended to preserve our safety. As adults we preserve and use these approaches even though time and time again we are unsuccessful in our attempts to arrive at satisfactory solutions to our interpersonal conflicts. Our strategies for resolving conflicts can be classified into four basic types: flight, diversion, fighting, and constructiveness. Figure #7 illustrates that flight is at one extreme while the constructive approach is at the other.

FIGURE #7

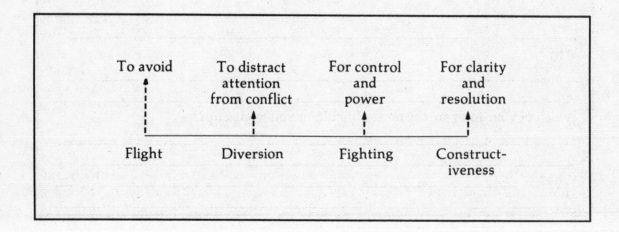

- How was conflict and anger dealt with in your family?
- Who was in control?
- Was it your mother or father who won the majority of the time?
- Think of one time in your family when a conflict was happily resolved.
- When your mother was angry at you, what was her favorite expression?
- When your father became angry at you, did he usually yell at you?
- When you are in conflict with your partner, what do you do?
- How do you express your anger?

1. Flight

Some people seem to run away at the first sign of conflict.

EXAMPLE

Sherry and Ralph have been married for two years. Sherry has some longstanding disagreements she wants to settle with Ralph, but he has been avoiding discussing them.

Sherry: Whenever I want to talk about anything that might create conflict between us you hide behind your newspaper or your work.

Ralph: I'm sorry Sherry but I can't talk about this right now, I've got a meeting.

Sherry: ARRGH! That's exactly what I mean!

Ralph: Sorry dear, have to go, see you later.

People who have a pattern of fleeing from conflict find all kinds of rational explanations for their behavior. They quit jobs because their bosses are incompetent. They get divorced because they weren't meant for each other. They are usually afraid to face up to conflicts, and they don't have the skills to do so. "I guess," and "I don't know," are common phrases these people use. They will do anything to avoid new situations because they have a great many doubts and fears about their competency as a result of fleeing from the unknown. Some couples flee into silence by making an unspoken agreement to not talk about any contentious issue as a way of avoiding conflict so they can have a "nice" (but boring) relationship.

There are situations where flight is the most appropriate and effective strategy. If your partner beats you up physically or verbally, the best thing to do is get away as quickly as possible. Sometimes it is also more effective to wait until a better time to deal with the conflict. For example, at a dinner party Bob disagrees with Sue's version of why her parents were recently divorced. It would be best if Bob didn't say anything until they got home to avoid a heated discussion in public.

2. Diversion

Diversion is an attempt to delay undesirable action by deflecting attention away from the conflict. Arguing over semantics, Changing the subject, and criticizing your partner's use of language are all tactics designed to divert attention away from the real problems or to keep the issues so unclear that attempts to constructively resolve the conflict are impossible.

EXAMPLE

Rex: You were late again last night; I want to know what's going on; this is five nights in a row.

Sara: What do you mean?

Rex: Look, you usually get home by 6:30, lately it's 10:30 or 11:30. I'm concerned that you might be seeing someone.

Sara: Oh, Rex, there you go again. Did the Freisons call about Saturday night?

Rex: I'm serious Sara, I'm not usually the jealous type and I still haven't got a straight answer from you.

Sara: O.K., if you're so worried I'll try to be home earlier tomorrow. Does that satisfy you?

Rex: No, and I think you're not going to deal with me directly.

Sara: I think you're making a mountain out of a molehill. Have you been working too hard again? Are you still seeing that shrink?

Sara's diversionary tactics are designed to keep Rex at bay. These kinds of tactics usually lead to feelings of dissatisfaction and anxiety in the partner who is being put off. Diversion can be a useful technique if you sense you are in danger or are trying to buy some time to straighten out your own thoughts in preparation for future action. As a general strategy, though, diversion leads to feelings such as fear of intimacy, paranoia, and stress. Eventually other people will give up on you in frustration.

3. Fighting

When in doubt, attack. This is the strategy adopted by some people in the face of conflict. The intention is to get power over the other by use of physical force (a punch in the nose); verbal assaults (screaming, yelling, long barrages of sentences); or punishment, both overt and covert (withholding love, sex, money, taking away privileges until the other gives in). Often one person will fight while the other flees. If both people fight then the couple's relationship will be characterized by vicious verbal attacks on hurtful subjects, shows of physical aggression in which objects get thrown around but no one is injured, great theatrical displays of outrageous behavior in public, and arguing about the same things over and over again. Fighting can also be carried on in a very rational way in which neither party shows any emotion or vulnerability, but each "cuts the other to ribbons" with cryptic comments perfectly timed to do the most damage to the other's self-esteem.

In any particular conflict, there is a winner and a loser. Wins, however, are only short term as the loser gathers force for revenge as soon as possible. Hostility, anger, anxiety, alienation, and physical damage are the usual by-products of these win-lose power tactics.

Flight, diversion, and fighting are the most common methods couples use in conflict situations; indeed, those methods are employed most often in the business world as well. There is another way to deal with conflict that takes more time initially but in the long run leads to greater payoffs.

4. Constructiveness

When you take a constructive approach to conflict, you try to resolve the disagreement with actions that are mutually satisfying to everyone involved. The constructive approach requires that you learn and practice a set of skills:

(a) The ability to figure out the source of the conflict

(b) An ability and willingness to initiate constructive action

(c) The ability to use the process of conversation (see chapter 5)

(d) The discipline to engage in a problem-solving process to bring about mutually acceptable action

It is also important that you develop the attitude that anything worthwhile doing is worth doing poorly the first few times you try. That is, your skills will grow in leaps and bounds if you try many times, succeed sometimes, and learn from your mistakes.

(a) Diagnosing the sources of conflict

When diagnosing the source and type of conflict, the most important issue is determining whether the conflict is a *value conflict*, a *real conflict*, or both. Almost all conflicts between couples are value conflicts or disagreements that reflect internal values, or the assumptions about what is "proper." For example, arguments over what love is, how much sex is enough, where to spend money, who should pick up the kids or take out the garbage, and when the stove should be cleaned, are all value based. There are no right answers to these conflicts. How they get worked out, however, will have a very significant impact on how much love, intimacy, and companionship you will experience in your relationship.

You do not have to change your values to arrive at a mutually acceptable resolution. You will, though, have to examine your intentions. If you take the stance of "It's my way or the highway," you will never have a loving, satisfying relationship. In a successful relationship, both partners are willing to be influenced by the other. If you do experience the feeling that you are losing yourself, examine your assumptions. You'll probably discover that you give yourself away too quickly in order to feel secure.

It is impossible to resolve conflicts unless everyone involved is willing to risk engaging in the process. In this case you will have to make an independent decision about how you are going to handle the conflict. That means you will have to find a way to disengage from the unproductive conflict.

(b) Initiating constructive action

If both of you are willing to be open to discussion and intend to resolve the conflict, use the process of constructive action outlined in the following example.

> *Joan:* I have a problem, are you willing to talk about it?
>
> *Gord:* Yes, I am willing.

(Both people set aside all possible distractions, sit facing each other in preparation for a serious discussion the same way they would for an important business meeting.)

> *Joan:* Gord, I've been telling you about this book I'm reading and how I think we could use it to clear up some problems in our relationship. I've asked you a couple of times to read it so we can discuss it, but you seem uninterested.

(Joan intentionally stops talking now so she doesn't overload Gord, who is likely to be a bit defensive. Even if he isn't defensive, it gives him a chance to reply. A key in discussing conflicted topics is to go slowly.)

> *Gord:* I don't like that pop-psych, self-improvement stuff, I don't think it does much good. Besides I don't think we have as many problems as you say we do; that's what happens when you read that stuff.

(Joan takes some deep breaths to calm herself because an angry outburst at this point would be ineffective. Even though she'd like to "kill him," she's going to keep her intention in mind.)

Joan: We have had four angry fights in the last two weeks. I am unhappy in this relationship. I think we need to improve our communications before it's too late. I would like you to give it a try with this book.

A defensive reaction to the initiation is quite common. It is important to discipline yourself to let it go for the moment otherwise your feelings will sidetrack you from your intended purpose. The most effective way to confront your partner is to go slowly, make short statements, and state the tangible effects the unresolved conflict is having on you. And breathe, breathe, breathe.

(c) Engaging in the process of communication

Engaging means listening, expressing yourself clearly and directly, being aware of and checking out your assumptions/understandings, being conscious of your feelings, keeping track of your intentions, and later on moving toward solutions to the conflict. Let's continue the conversation between Joan and Gord.

Gord: So, unless I read this book you're going to take off.

Joan: No, I didn't say I was going to take off. I was trying to tell you that I think we have some communication problems and I believe this book could help. I would really appreciate it if you would give it a try.

(Gord feels less defensive, and now open to the discussion. He understands what is happening and responds.)

Gord: You think we have some communication problems and you would appreciate my giving it a try.

Joan: Yes, that's what I said. Basically I think we have a pretty good relationship and if we learned how to handle our con-

flicts better we'd both be happier.

Gord: You think basically we have a good relationship. You just want us to learn how to deal with our conflicts better. Geez, I thought it was the end and you were ready to go out the door.

Joan: I heard you say you thought I was ready to leave you. (Gord, acknowledges with a nod).

Gord: Okay. I'm willing to give it a try. What did you have in mind?

Joan and Gord are well on their way to searching for some ways to resolve their conflict. Gord was open to the discussion, which helped a lot. Joan's willingness to discipline herself and not harangue Gord helped too. Although this is a simple example that may seem too easy, it shows how both people can learn to deal effectively with conflicts.

(d) Problem solving

The final skill in the constructive approach is to search for possible solutions to the conflict and agree to try one out. The first step is to clarify the problem. What needs to be changed? What is each person's opinion about the perceived need for change? Joan has clarified her problem; she thinks they don't communicate very well. She wants them to learn how to communicate better, which will require time. Gord will also read the book, or at least parts of it. Gord is willing to give it a try.

The second step is to generate and evaluate a number of possible solutions. Let's return again to the conversation between Joan and Gord.

Joan: I would like you to read the book, then we can discuss it.

Gord: You want me to read the book. (Joan nods in agreement.) I don't enjoy reading these kinds of books and I'm likely to never finish it. You read it to me.

106

Joan: You don't think you'll read the book and you want me to read it to you. (Gord says, "Yes, that's what I said.") I somehow don't think that will work, I would feel like I was doing all the work and a bit like I was the teacher. I think you would find the chapter on the six stages interesting, how about you reading that, then we can talk, okay?

Gord: I heard you say that if you read the book to me you would feel like the teacher and you don't want that. You think I would be interested in reading the chapter on the stages, then we can talk about it. (Joan agrees.)

The next steps are to mutually agree on a workable solution and to make definite plans for implementing the solution, including when, where, and how.

Gord: Okay. I'll read the chapter. Let's see, today is Monday. I'll finish it by Friday, then we can talk about it Saturday evening.

Joan: You'll read the chapter by Friday and we'll talk Saturday. (Gord agrees.)

Gord: Oh, one more thing, I want you to agree to not bug me about whether or not I'm reading it. If you do that I'm likely to get angry and not do it. That's what I did when my mother bugged me about my homework.

Joan: (chuckling) I heard you say that you want me to not bug you about reading the chapter, otherwise you might get angry and not do it. You did that when your mother bugged you about homework.

Gord: Yes.

While it may seem tedious to keep repeating to your partner what you heard, it is crucial for maintaining the clarity in your exchanges. This is particularly true for contentious issues. It helps to slow the process, which will keep the conversation on a rational basis.

The final step is to evaluate the solution and make any necessary changes. One way of doing this is the P.I.T. method created by Dr. John Jones. After trying out the solution, each person takes turns making statements about three areas:

(a) *Personal* — what you learned by doing it and how you personally are feeling at this time

(b) *Interpersonal* — what you think and how you feel about your partner now

(c) *Task* — how well you think the experiment went; what, if anything, needs to be changed; and finally, making an agreement about what to do next, and when

5. The Mack truck syndrome

The constructive approach to conflict is, of course, the most effective in the long run. If you learn the skills at home you can use them to great advantage to yourself and your coworkers in the workplace as well.

The ability and willingness to resolve your conflicts is essential to your feeling happy and satisfied in all your relationships. Learning to deal effectively with anger is crucial to the successful resolution of conflict, as it is the single most potent obstacle in this process.

A final note on the effects of conflict: After a particularly "heavy" round of conflict that rocks the very foundations of a relationship, we experience what we call the Mack truck syndrome. After we've resolved our differences we often feel we've become closer but our bodies are jolted like we've been run over by a Mack truck. It eventually goes away and, in fact, we feel a higher level of energy a few days later. We're not sure of the origins of the feelings, we just recognize that we experience them sometimes. We find taking deep breaths helps a lot

b. DEALING WITH ANGER

Anger is one of the first and most frightening emotions we experience. It is the emotion a child feels when he or she cries for food; it is the emotion parents use to punish their children; it is the fuel for verbal and physical abuse in families; it is the most prevalent emotion seen in human relations. Anger in its most perverse form, hatred, has destroyed millions of lives. It is also the most misunderstood emotion in our society.

1. Here comes the judge

Anger and its variations (rage, resentment, irritation, annoyance, criticism, sarcasm, cynicism, indifference, coldness, verbal and physical violence, sadness, impatience) are central themes in everyday life. Your attitudes toward anger reflect your world view. If you want to discover the politics of your relationship, take a look at how you and your partner deal with anger. In relationships we often rationalize anger and become self-righteous. In our counseling practice, when couples come to see us in anger, one or both of them is usually self-righteous about their anger. They look to us to justify that self-righteousness so they can feel good and make the partner feel bad.

The mythology of anger, more than any other emotion, is a story of trial and judgment, or crime and punishment. You are the kangaroo court in which indictment and argument, verdict and sentence are all played out without any real say from the accused. Anger is a direct and clear reflection of your unexamined personal values, expectations, and assumptions. The more unaware you are of yourself, the more angry you will be.

Anger, whether expressed or kept inside, is our insistence upon having things our own way, whether that insistence is based on so-called self-assertiveness or infantile obstinacy, rather than any deep commitment to those ideals. So we get angry at trivia in order to assert our stubborn demand for independence.

2. The anatomy of anger

Anger is not necessarily destructive; it's what you do with it that creates the problems. We think anger can actually be a vehicle to intimacy and love. In order for this to happen, though, you must learn how to move through and beyond anger. Unfortunately for most people in this society, anger is associated with separation and alienation. Most couples get trapped in becoming more and more angry, either by withdrawing or by expressing it through verbal barrages or physical violence.

Anger is a secondary emotion. For all its importance and impact, anger is a lesser emotion than empathy, love, grief, fear, and joy. It is a reaction to the fundamental emotion of fear. Figure #8 illustrates how

ACTIVITY #26
SELF-AWARENESS

Stand in front of a mirror looking at yourself. Now get REALLY ANGRY at the person in the mirror! Do all the usual things you do when you get angry: yell, sulk, pout, punish, glare, point your finger at the accused, name-call, lecture, etc. Do this until you can't stand it anymore. This is how you look from the other side.

108

anger is generated and how it spirals in intensity. Like a tornado, the spiral of anger can cause major disasters until all its energy is dissipated and calm is restored. Often in its wake, trust and goodwill are damaged or permanently destroyed.

We get angry when we think some external event might be threatening to us, or when we experience the frustration of unmet expectations. It could be a word (e.g., wimp, immature, impotent, frigid), a phrase (e.g., put the dishes away, you never help around here, don't do that, not tonight dear), or an action (e.g., walking away, sticking out your tongue, a hand on a buttock). As the perception of the threat is formed, we make unconscious assumptions about the potential danger of that threat. If we conclude that the threat is not very great, or that we are powerful enough to confront it successfully, we can respond calmly. But if we conclude that the threat is too much, we are overwhelmed with fear, which shows in such bodily reactions as increased heart rate, sweating, panic, rapid breathing, and increased muscular activity. Finally a burst of anger pours forth in an attempt to destroy or reduce the perceived threat and protect our assumed helplessness. All of these activities usually go on outside of our awareness. If someone points out to us that we're angry, we'll often deny it.

Curiously, anger seems to be a response to something outside of us, but in fact, is an intra-personal event. We make ourselves angry. But because anger is so unpleasant, we try to get rid of it by putting it on those around us. We identify the source of our anger as being outside ourselves, which is an attempt to get away from the experience

FIGURE #8

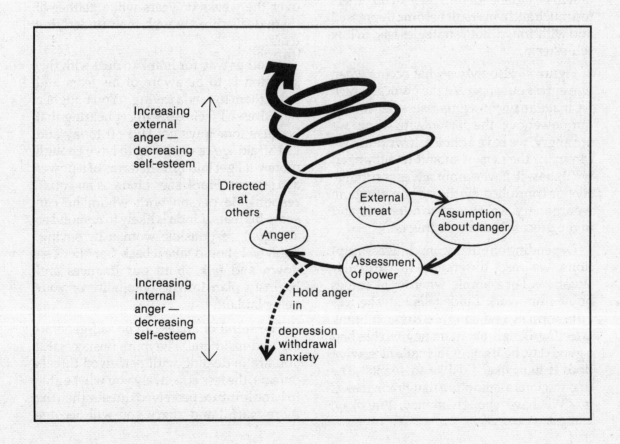

of fear. We say, "You make me angry," or "You're so obnoxious!"

The other thing we might say when we have difficulty dealing with our anger is "You're angry!" But what we really mean is, "I'm angry at you." This reflects a fear of our own anger and an attempt to put it on the other person. This is called projection; it's like throwing a hot potato to someone else because it's too hot to handle ourselves. With enough persistence, the other partner can wind up being angry over the persistence, not the original accusation, and the spiral gains energy.

Fear is always underneath anger. The more fear you have, but are unwilling to acknowledge, the more anger you will direct at others. Your disowned fears feed your anger. If your anger is chronically explosive it means that you have a great fear of exploring how dependent you are on others. If you consistently keep your anger inside, you probably are very reluctant to be independent. You lean on others too much and as a result become depressed and withdrawn. Both strategies lead to low self-esteem.

Figure #8 also shows what occurs when we repress our anger. At the point at which we make an unconscious assessment about our power over the person with whom we are angry, we have a choice. If we think we can make the person submit to our anger, we'll show it. If we see ourselves as submissive or controlled by the person at whom we are angry, we'll keep it to ourselves, and in the process become depressed.

Depending on our unconscious assumptions, we react differently to particular situations. For example, when Frank comes home from work, Linda tells him she was out shopping and bought a dress. If Frank is feeling all right about money and has had a good day, he'll say, "Oh, that's nice, what does it look like? I'd like to see it." The unconscious assumption that Frank makes is, "We have enough money, I'm okay;

there's no threat." But if Linda tells Frank that she bought a new dress, and Frank has just heard about four people being laid off and he's worrying about money, he's likely to yell at her, "What have you done that for!? You are always spending money! You never think about how I have to earn it! What am I supposed to do? How can I keep up with your wasting all my money!?" Linda, of course would be taken aback by Frank's outrage because she doesn't know what's going on inside of him. On the anger spiral Frank has perceived a threat but he doesn't say that to Linda. The next thing he assumes, in terms of power, is that he must get her under control so that she doesn't start spending too much money, and the quickest way to do that is to get angry because when he gets angry Linda gets scared and watches her step. *All of this occurs outside of Frank's awareness.* Linda may get her anger out indirectly by going out and buying more things to assert her independence. Their ensuing fights escalate over the weeks or years while neither of them deals directly with their underlying fears.

Another way for Frank to deal with this situation is to be aware of his fears and voice them to Linda saying, "You bought a new dress? I feel really upset hearing that because four guys got laid off today and I'm afraid we're not going to have enough money if I get laid off." In terms of a power assessment, Frank sees Linda as an equal, responsible person with whom he can share his fears. Linda is likely to respond as an equal, responsible woman by saying, "Maybe I should take it back." or "Let's sit down and talk about our finances and begin to plan for the possibility of your being laid off."

The spiral of anger can be self-generating and insidious. The more unsuccessful you are in dealing with perceived threats or fears, the less effectively you will be able to handle future perceived threats, then the more fearful and angry you will become

ACTIVITY #27
THINKING ABOUT ANGER

Think about the last few times you were angry.

When you get angry, where in your body do you feel it?

_____
_____
_____
_____

What does it feel like?

_____
_____
_____

Do you hold anger in or explode?

_____
_____
_____

How does that make you feel?

_____
_____
_____
_____

When someone gets angry at you, how do you react?

_____
_____
_____

How does that make you feel?

_____
_____
_____
_____

Whose anger do you fear the most?

_____
_____
_____

For the next week, you and your partner keep a record of your angry outbursts. Watch to see whether you can chart your internal thoughts that precede an angry outburst. Be aware of when you are afraid, even just a little bit. Listen very carefully to yourself when you are even a little frustrated. Are you authoritarian or compromising? Do you "beat around the bush" or are you like a bull in a china shop?

You can use the following questions to map your anger patterns.

- What time of day did the angry outburst occur?

- With whom were you angry?

- What was the event that triggered your anger?

- What did you do when you were angry?

- Is there a pattern to your behavior?

- What tone of your voice did you use?

- What body gestures did you use?

- Did you show your anger to some people and hold it in when others were nearby?

- How did you feel after you were angry?

- What were the reactions of others to your anger — especially your partner, your children, and your coworkers?

- When you have recorded several angry outbursts using the above questions, try doing something that you think might help you create a better outcome.

about them. Because you haven't examined your assumptions, you begin to lose touch with reality by creating fears that seem real but under closer scrutiny are not. When threatened you grab for your most potent weapon, which is anger. Over time you know you don't get what you want by getting angry because the people around you withdraw from you. You also feel unable to handle life effectively. You try to hide these doubts from others, but you know inside what's going on. All of this builds a feeling of insecurity and low self-esteem. You then become threatened or fearful even more easily and the spiral

of anger grows as you become impossible to live with. *The root of anger is fear and to break the cycle you must examine your fears, doubts, and worries.*

The same process occurs if you hold in your anger. You become depressed, more fearful, doubting, and withdrawn. To break that downward cycle you must, in a safe, understanding environment, look over the edge of your fears to see what's there so you can begin to take the necessary action to move beyond your fears.

Each individual in a relationship has to address his or her own internal issue of fear and how it contributes to anger. It is probably one of the most important factors involved in whether or not a relationship will survive because anger blocks the resolution of conflict. You must learn to recognize the origins of anger and take steps to move beyond it.

A useful way of learning how to deal effectively with your anger is to find out what you've learned about anger in the past. Try Activity #29.

3. Healthy versus destructive anger

One of the reasons people have difficulty dealing with anger is that sometimes, when someone gets angry, it feels just right or legitimate. You know this person takes you seriously. Other times when someone is angry, it doesn't feel right. You feel mistreated, misunderstood, or punished. The difficulty is learning to tell the difference between what we call *healthy* anger, which is the kind of anger that has a real basis to it, and *destructive* anger, which is used to control and manipulate. Destructive anger is irresponsible and can lead to verbal and physical violence.

Destructive anger has no particular basis in the reality of day-to-day exchanges, conversations, or events. It's just there. Your life becomes more and more dissatisfying whether you are the object of the anger or the person who is angry. It's very difficult to deal with because the source of anger can't be pinned down. Destructive anger is a smoke screen covering fears, and is used as a control and an abuse of power over the partner and other family members.

Healthy anger, on the other hand, arises out of broken agreements that have been previously negotiated or when a mutual expectation is not fulfilled. Healthy anger is connected to a particular, identifiable issue; by addressing the reasons for the anger, the relationship becomes clearer. For instance, suppose you make a date to meet your partner downtown at a certain place and at an agreed upon time. You

arrive but your partner doesn't. You wait for an hour but she doesn't show. You are angry. You later find out that your partner forgot that she was supposed to meet you. Your anger is healthy because it is tied to an agreement that your partner has broken. It means that you hold your partner accountable and you have enough self-esteem to know that you are a person who expects others to show their caring by keeping their agreements. If your partner cares about you she will respect and listen to your anger and make sure she doesn't do it again. Underneath your anger is still fear, probably the fear that she doesn't care enough about you to show up on time.

If you are prepared and know how to handle anger well, fights can lead to a deeper relationship. One effective way of learning how to deal with your anger is to reflect on your internal responses to anger through the use of directed fantasy. Fantasy is simply setting some time aside by yourself, to think about your attitudes, behaviors, and issues in your life. The anger fantasy in Activity #30 is a self-examination to help you find some effective ways of dealing with your anger.

Be aware of how you feel. What is your level of satisfaction with the events in the fantasy? Were you satisfied with your reaction? How did the other person react to you? Take three deep breaths, then continue on to Part 2.

How are you feeling now? What was your level of satisfaction with your actions? If you feel unsatisfied, that's okay. You can return to this fantasy as many times as you wish to help yourself deal with your own personal anger. Each time you do it you will become a little bit better at handling your anger in a more loving way.

As a way of learning more from this experience, go on to Part 3 of this activity.

Now write out a list of your fears that lead to your getting angry. What do you think you have to learn about your anger?

ACTIVITY #29
YOUR ANGER BELIEFS

Write down the first thing that comes to your mind when you read the following phrases. Try to be honest with yourself to gain the most from this activity.

When people get mad, they should _____

Feeling angry is _____

The last time I got angry I _____

Then I felt _____

People who get angry are _____

When I get angry, I _____

I get angry at people when _____

I'm afraid that _____

I get angry at myself when _____

I'm afraid that _____

When my father got angry, he _____

As a child, that made me feel _____

When my mother got angry she _____

As a child, that made me feel _____

If I didn't get angry so much, I might _____

I don't show my anger to _____

With regard to my anger, I'd like to learn _____

Right now I'm feeling _____

Take some time to review what you've written, think about what you've learned and how that might help you get a better handle on your anger.

Find a quiet place that is protected from any intrusions. Sit in a comfortable chair or couch, take six very deep breaths and relax. Read slowly. If you feel uncomfortable doing this, just observe your discomfort. Take one more deep breath.

Imagine this little scene: You are in a room with another person, and a topic comes up for discussion. As the person is talking you realize you're becoming angry. You also realize that you are going to express it or repress it.

- What do you do?

- What do you say?

- Who is this person?

- How are you expressing or repressing your anger?

- What kinds of thoughts pass through your mind?

- What are you feeling in your body?

Allow this fantasy to complete itself before reading on.

Write down two or three guidelines that will help you to deal more successfully with your anger. What, for you, would be the most difficult and positive thing to do that would help you move from destructive, angry reactions to more satisfying exchanges. Write that down.

Are you willing to commit yourself to changing your behavior so that you can move beyond your anger? If you are, what help do you need to do that well? If you're not willing, why not?

4. Anger and self-assertion

Chronic anger can take the place of self-assertion. An angry person may use anger as a way of avoiding stating directly what he or she wants, while attacking the partner for not coming across with it.

EXAMPLE

Sam wants to have sex with Gina but he doesn't ask her if she is interested. He snuggles up to her a bit but never states what he has in mind; nothing happens. The next day Sam stomps around the house criticizing Gina for everything she does. Sam is using anger to try and punish Gina for not giving him what he didn't ask for. Rather than be assertive, he gets angry at her by being critical, punitive, and demanding perfection. He might, if he has the opportunity, become judgmental and call her frigid.

If you consistently allow someone to vent their destructive anger on you, you are showing a problem with self-assertion because you are not confronting their destructive anger or objecting to being mistreated. The consequence of not asserting yourself will be loss of self-respect, self-confidence, and a sense of overwhelming helplessness. Your assertion may come in two forms. First, you can confront your partner about his or her destructive anger

Again, imagine that you are in the room with the same person as in your previous fantasy. The same thing begins to happen: you're having a disagreement; you feel yourself becoming angry.

But this time, as you begin to feel your anger rising, you stop and think about what you might be afraid of. You take a couple of deep breaths. You find a way of dealing with your anger through which you are going to feel more satisfied. You have the wisdom and experience to do it; you just have to let yourself tap into that wise part of yourself.

Let your mind concentrate on finding a response that will be satisfactory for both of you — one with which you feel closer to each other. When you feel finished with the fantasy, silently say to the person, "Thank you for helping me to find out more about my anger."

When you're ready, end the fantasy. Take a deep breath.

and the effect it's having on you, then demand specific changes in behavior. If this strategy doesn't work, you will have to remove yourself from your partner as a way of asserting yourself.

Let's continue with the example of Sam and Gina.

EXAMPLE

Gina finally figures out what's going on with Sam and decides to confront him.

Gina: Look Sam, I think you're criticizing me and punishing me. My guess is that it has something to do with last night. Did you want to have sex with me and now you're angry because it didn't happen?

Sam: Well, you're never interested in sex!

Gina: (Directly, with determination, not anger) Sam, that is not true. If you want something from me I want you to ask directly. It doesn't mean you'll always get

what you want but if you don't ask, you'll never get what you want.

Sam: Sometimes I feel too embarrassed to ask, like I shouldn't or like I'm a little boy asking for a cookie from my mommy. I'll try though.

Gina: You may feel embarrassed, but unless you take the risk, you're always going to blame me. I think it's going to require more than trying; I think you will have to just do it. When you punish me I don't want to have anything to do with you.

Sam: I will try, I'm surprised how afraid I am to ask for what I want, especially from you, the one person it should be easy with. That was difficult for me; thanks for the feedback.

The encounter would have gone another way if Sam had adopted a defensive, angry posture. If he was chronically defensive,

Take a pen and paper and write down the alternative ways you considered acting when you were angry. How did you act in the first fantasy? Were you satisfied? Was there anything in the second fantasy that was more satisfying to you? If so, why? If not, write down an alternative that might be more satisfying.

Gina would at some point have to make a decision about whether she was going to take the abuse. Gina is obviously the kind of person who won't tolerate it for long. Sam probably knows that and respects her, so responds to her confronting him. It also speaks well of his willingness and ability to take in feedback.

If you have a pattern of being angry or freely critical of others, you must learn how to listen. You likely focus on others to justify your angry behavior. You spend too much time being angry or talking to others in an angry authoritative manner. As a result you probably think your relationships are in better shape than they really are. People who have to be physically close to you have withdrawn psychologically from you by not talking to you or being very careful about what they say to you, or they will tell you what they think you want to hear. If you do begin to listen to others you will hear a lot of things that will be difficult for you to take in or agree with. But listen you must if you ever hope to develop a satisfying relationship. Does this description fit you or your partner? If so, try activity #33.

5. Dealing with others' anger

When a parent uses anger to punish a child by yelling or withdrawing love, the child experiences terror. The more destructive anger a child sees, the more terror he or she experiences. Every parent uses destructive anger to control and punish their child at one time. Thus, we carry the fear of being yelled at, or the fear of the stoney, angry silence into our adult life. You can respond to somebody else's anger by becoming angry yourself or by being completely swamped by fear. Either way the anger remains unresolved.

Learning how to effectively handle someone else's anger is a skill that you need to develop to feel more competent in interpersonal relations. The prerequisite is that you be aware of your own fears about anger, your attitudes about anger, and the behaviors you engage in when you are angry.

If you regard another person's anger as threatening, you'll start the spiral of anger operating in yourself. Then you will have your own anger to deal with as well as the other's. To get angry just because another person is angry is to give in to your own fears that you have about anger. In many relationships, anger is like a contagious disease that spreads like the flu. Fighting anger with anger can also mean that you adopt the other person's style of relating, which can leave you frustrated, exhausted, and feeling bad about yourself.

There are some steps we think you will find useful when dealing with someone else's anger directed at you. These steps will work only when both people want to

Give the description of anger in the paragraph in the first column on page 117 to a friend, spouse, or your child. Ask them to read it to see if it comes close to describing you.

Listen carefully to the person's feedback. If you find yourself becoming defensive, breathe deeply and listen. Thank the person for their feedback and think about what they've said for two days before you discuss it with them. You might consider doing the same thing with another person.

If you fit the description above, take out paper and a pencil and rewrite it replacing "you" with "I." For example, "I have a pattern of being angry and critical of others. I focus on others..." Add to the description of yourself. This will help you become more self-aware and begin taking responsibility for your anger and underlying fears that fuel your anger.

move past anger to clearer communications.

(a) Acknowledge that the other person is angry. Often we'll try to talk the person out of his or her anger by saying, "Oh, you're not really angry" or, "You'll get over it, it's not a big deal." We do that because we are afraid of their anger. Acknowledgment of anger shows that you see what is happening and are willing to respond.

(b) Recognize how and when your own fears and defenses come into play. If someone is angry at you, you may find yourself becoming very sensitive and distorting what they are saying. Or you may blow the amount of anger they are expressing out of proportion. Before you respond to anger, take four or five deep breaths, count to twenty-two, and think about what your intentions are in responding. You might even consider not responding to the anger. If you don't know what to say, you might try, "I don't know what to say," and just leave it at that, or "I need some time to think about what

you've said," or, "I think if I say anything right now, you're going to be more angry at me. I'd be willing to talk to you when you've calmed down and are ready to listen."

(c) If you are willing to continue the exchange, clarify what is really going on from your perspective. Give some specific feedback to your partner. For example, "You seem to be really angry at me right now. I need to know what you are angry about, because I don't understand."

(d) Find out what the other person wants from you. Say, "I don't know what you want; tell me," or, "Tell me what you expect me to do."

(e) Talk together about the part each of you has played in the angry exchange. It may be that only one person has caused the rift, but it takes two to untangle it.

(f) Mutually agree on how you can handle similar situations in the future. For example, "If I'm going to be late for a meeting with you, I will phone you," or, "Don't criticize me when I'm busy; wait until we both have time to deal with it adequately," or, "When things start heating up and we're in a hurry to go somewhere, we'll wait until we have more time to talk."

(g) Be willing to genuinely admit your mistakes or misinterpretations by saying, "I'm sorry, I didn't understand how it affected you," or, "You're right, I was really inconsiderate." Or, if you think the other person's anger has nothing to do with you, let them know by saying, "I think your anger has nothing to do with me," or, "It seems to me you have a lot of anger and I think something else is bothering you."

(h) Be willing to forgive yourself and your partner for what you have and haven't done. This doesn't mean forgiving and forgetting. Nor does forgiving mean that you have to condone your partner's actions. It means that you can learn from your mistakes and move on. At the same time, you must be willing to hold yourself and your partner accountable for your mutual agreements that have come out of the exchange.

(i) If you can't arrive at an agreement about the anger, call in a friend, or go to a counselor to work out your differences and resolve the anger that may be growing between you. Anger doesn't disappear just because you are unable or unwilling to deal with it. It's like the grass on the front lawn in summer; it keeps growing and growing, and the longer you put off dealing with it, the harder it is to handle.

You can learn to use anger to deepen your intimacy. It does require discipline, a willingness to speak truthfully, plus two people who are willing and able to acknowledge and explore their fears.

6. Breaking the anger spiral

At some time in your relationship you will have a "knock-'em-down-drag-'em-out" screaming match in which both of you blow your tops. There will also be times when you get angry simultaneously. The stronger your feelings, the less likely you will have clear communications. When you both get angry there are just two ideas, two feelings, two judgments spiralling around in space. You can be sure neither of you is listening to the other.

To break the spiral of anger you must step out of it, stop the verbal barrages, and agree to listen, even though both of you are feeling highly charged. The next time you get into an argument with your partner, friend, or child, call a truce, stop talking, take eight or nine deep breaths, and search for a way to find some common ground in your argument. Sometimes it's useful to wait an hour or two, perhaps a whole day, before you begin to deal with your issues more rationally and constructively. When you can both agree to talk about it you *must* institute the following rule: *each person can speak for him or herself only after accurately restating what each heard the partner say.* Before presenting your own point of view, it will be necessary for you to acknowledge what your partner has said. You should understand his or her thoughts and feelings so well, you are able to summarize them for him or her. It will also slow down the rate of exchange so that each of you can think before you speak. Sounds simple doesn't it? It is simple if you discipline yourself to breathe and listen. It is difficult if you are anxious to blurt out everything at once.

This procedure is absolutely essential if you ever hope to break the spiral of your mutual anger. If you doubt the validity of the method, the next time you have an argument, turn on your audio cassette machine and record your fight, then listen to it. How does your exchange compare with the following?

We recently had a verbal fight during which we broke every rule in the book. Each of us retreated to our favorite pouting places in the house — Judy to the bedroom and Jim to his office. We were continuing the argument in our head when we left each other — a classic case of "My way or the highway!" We both realized how ridiculous it was for both of us to be alone and miserable. We decided to start over again and to follow the rules of listening and breathing this time.

Judy: I want to talk to you about the party we went to last evening. I felt annoyed at what happened.

Jim: I heard you say that you want to talk about the party last night and you're really angry at me.

Judy: That's partially correct. I said that I'm annoyed at you about what happened.

Jim: I heard you say that you're annoyed at me for what happened.

Judy: Yes, that's correct.

Jim: I don't know what you're so annoyed about. I had a good time at the party, and it was fine as far as I'm concerned.

Judy: I heard you say that you don't understand what it is that I'm annoyed about. You thought the evening was fine.

Jim: Right.

Judy: Well, I'm angry because I felt that as soon as we arrived at the party you went off and I didn't see you for the rest of the night. I felt like you ignored me and left me.

Jim: I heard you say that when we got to the party, I just went off and you didn't see me for the rest of the night.

Judy: And I also felt you ignored me.

Jim: You think I was ignoring you.

Judy: Yes, that's right.

Jim: I don't think I was ignoring you, and I don't think I went off for the whole evening. I came back to check with you a few times, to see if you wanted a drink or not. You seemed to be talking to other people and having an enjoyable time.

Judy: So, I hear you saying that you don't think that you did ignore me purposely, and that I seemed to be enjoying myself talking with other people. (Judy feels her anger rising in her stomach and chest, so takes a few deep breaths to maintain her cool and keep on track.)

Jim: Yes. (Jim observing Judy's edge of anger, feels his defensiveness rise, but takes a few deep breaths so that he doesn't give in to the impulse. He knows, from experience, that if he follows his impulse, a fight will surely follow.)

Judy: Well, I thought differently. I don't like it when you spend most of the evening talking to other people. From my perspective, you didn't spend any of the evening talking with me, other than a few moments here and there. (Judy stops, realizing she's getting steamed up and that Jim is going to have a hard time taking it all in if she gets going.)

Jim: I heard you say that you don't like it when I spend most of the evening talking to others, and I forgot what else you said. Would you please repeat it.

Judy: That you just talked to me here and there for a moment.

Jim: And you don't like it when I just talk to you here and there for a moment.

Judy: That's right.

Jim: I didn't realize that. I didn't really. I wasn't deliberately ignoring you. It just wasn't my intention to do that. As I said, you seemed to be having a good time.

Judy: So, I hear you saying that you didn't realize that was bothering me; you just thought I was having a good time.

Jim: Yes.

Judy: What I would like to do is come to some kind of an agreement about what we'll do when we go to parties so we can avoid these misunderstandings. I would prefer you to spend more of the time with me than for me to just be left with other people I don't know.

Jim: What you would like to do is come to an agreement about what we are going to do when we go to these parties so you could spend more time with me.

Judy: Yes.

Jim: Okay. What if we spend time at the beginning orienting ourselves to the party atmosphere and staying together. If you or I see someone we want to talk with, we'll tell each other and do it together.

Judy: I heard you say that we will spend some time together getting oriented to the party. If we want to talk with someone, we'll do it together.

Jim: Yes.

Judy: That sounds good to me. I feel nervous when I first go to a party and when you go off I think you don't care about me.

Jim: I heard you agree with my proposal and that you feel nervous at the beginning of a party and that you think I don't care about you when I go off.

Judy: Yes.

Jim: I didn't realize that. Actually I feel nervous too, so I start mixing to cover my nervousness, then I get all caught up in it.

(We went on to talk about our reactions at parties and other situations, in which we were scared. The format allowed us to move beyond our anger and to develop more understanding and intimacy.)

Using this method is like putting money in the bank; your interest compounds and you've got resources set aside for any unexpected crisis that may come up.

Our experience working with thousands of people over the years in our private practice and couples workshops is that when they use the skills outlined in this chapter, they experience greatly reduced levels of anger, fear, distrust, and interpersonal tension. They move from anger to love, from confusion to clarity, and from chaos to peace of mind. You can, too, when you make these skills part of your everyday life.

c. BATTERED WOMEN, TERRIFIED CHILDREN: GETTING FREE OF MEN'S ANGER AND AGGRESSION

Tens of thousands of women and children are the objects of men's anger and aggression. Approximately 50% of all adult women will be battered at some time in their lives. It is estimated that 50 to 60% of all marriages today contain some violence. Women's injuries range from bruises, cuts, and sprains to broken bones and death. A battered woman is not usually the victim of a single abusive incident but is wrapped up in a spiral of anger and violence that involves physical, emotional, and sexual abuse. Angry, violent men are found in all communities, all cultures, and all income levels. They abuse women of all ages, particularly pregnant women.

Abusive men have intense, dependent relationships with their partners. They are excessively possessive and jealous and take extreme measures (including intimidation and violence) to control women. These men have difficulty expressing their personal needs or feelings and emotions, except for anger. They believe in male supremacy and have traditional ideas of male dominance in the family. In our experience working with angry, violent men, they are very difficult to influence and have a high level of distrust and defensiveness in the counseling situation.

If you are a woman who is being abused by your partner, this book will not be of much help to you. He is likely to react to the suggestions with defensiveness and anger, or perhaps more violence. The problem is not one of relationship. He must deal with his anger and aggression first, separate from you. He has a problem that requires long-term counseling. It is likely that the only way he is ever going to seek help is if you leave him. We recognize and understand that this course of action is probably going to be the most difficult one for you in the short run. There are some resources available to you. Find out if there is a transition house in your area by phoning the local women's resource center or social service agency. If you have friends or relatives you can rely on, go to them. If your relatives tell you to tough it out, don't listen to them; keep looking for ways out. Your decision to leave will be made difficult because each time your partner is violent with you, he will promise to never do it again and will be calm and loving for a while. This will lead you to doubt that it will happen again. If he does abuse you again, you must take action.

If you do leave your partner he will probably beg for your forgiveness and promise never to hit or threaten you again. He will try to convince you that he realizes that he has done wrong and now has changed. In our experience abusive, angry, violent men only change in a long-term program of counseling. The counseling should be a combination of individual sessions, plus group sessions led by a man or pair of men. Abusive men who enter counseling need the support, confrontation, and guidance of other men who have already begun to resolve their problems. At some time in the counseling he should attend an intensive residential program of at least one week, but preferably one month. In our opinion the best programs available anywhere are in PD Seminars, R.R. #1, Davis Road, Gabriola Island, British Columbia, Canada, V0R 1X0.

Angry, violent men will seek help only when they are in crisis, when they are helpless without female support. They rarely seek assistance unless their partner leaves them or they are ordered by the courts. Because men who go for help do so in a moment of crisis, they become impatient as the crisis passes and their resolve to change is easily weakened. It is important, then, that the man get help in the crisis and his partner not let him off the hook a few months later. She must remain insistent that he continue the counseling if he has any hope of reconciliation. Any resistance on his part is an indication of his inability or unwillingness to understand the depth of his problem. Even if he shows significant positive changes in his behavior in the short run she, and he, must stick with this program of counseling if those positive changes are to be incorporated into his everyday behavioral patterns. He must learn to not give in to his impatience and overly optimistic view of the situation. He has to learn self-discipline and how to deal with reality and this can only occur over a long period of time. Once he has dealt with his anger, violence, and aggression, it is possible to begin addressing the relationship issues.

Men's anger and violence is also directed at their children. Sexual abuse of children is one of the most disturbing of all family violence problems. About 75% of sexual abuse cases involve family members or adults well known to the family. The very environment in which the child should be able to find love, support, and comfort is the one in which he or she finds terror, anxiety, and pain. One in two females and one in three males are victims of unwanted sexual acts. About 90% of the children were under age 21 when the first offenses were committed against them. Four of every one hundred young females have been raped; three in five sexually abused children have been threatened or physically coerced by their assailants. Tragically, the child is often the one who is removed from the home while the abuser, usually an older male, remains in his community untreated and unchanged.

In our opinion, the depth and breadth of men's anger, aggression, and violence in this society is creating what we call "the other nuclear war," and the fallout is being felt by everyone. These are not relationship problems and cannot be addressed through marital or relationship counseling. These men will have to address their internal problems of helplessness, immaturity, insecurities, fears, and great emotional dependence on women before they can begin to have equal, loving relationships.

For more information about these issues contact the National Clearinghouse on Family Violence, Health and Welfare Canada, Ottawa, Canada, K1A 1B5, or Family Services Association of America, 44 East 23rd Street, New York, N.Y., 10010, or your local family service association in the Yellow Pages (under Associations).

ACTIVITY #34
SUMMARY: HOW WELL DO YOU HANDLE CONFLICT?

Do you fight, flee, or handle conflicts with your partner effectively? Check the response that outlines how you react to conflict with your partner.

1. When he or she gets angry at me I usually:
   - ❏ (a) Get angry back
   - ❏ (b) Try to persuade him or her to cool off
   - ❏ (c) Listen, analyze the situation, then state my view
   - ❏ (d) Leave, walk away

2. When I walk in on a fight my partner is having with someone, I'll probably:
   - ❏ (a) Jump in and take sides
   - ❏ (b) Try to mediate
   - ❏ (c) Quietly observe
   - ❏ (d) Get out of there

3. When I think that my partner is taking advantage of me, I:
   - ❏ (a) Tell him or her to stop
   - ❏ (b) Use persuasion and facts to stop it
   - ❏ (c) Change how I relate to him or her
   - ❏ (d) Let it ride

4. When I disagree with my partner, I typically:
   - ❏ (a) Try to get him or her to see my side
   - ❏ (b) Use logic to minimize the conflict
   - ❏ (c) Look for a compromise
   - ❏ (d) Avoid the issue altogether until it goes away

5. After an argument with my partner, I might:
   - ❏ (a) Try to convince him or her I'm right
   - ❏ (b) Attempt to work out our differences
   - ❏ (c) Not talk to him or her again for a day or three
   - ❏ (d) Not say anything about it again

6. When serious conflicts begin to arise between the two of us, I usually:
   - ❏ (a) Clearly and in no uncertain terms express my concerns
   - ❏ (b) Play referee
   - ❏ (c) Cautiously engage while watching to see what will happen
   - ❏ (d) Subtly withdraw, hoping it will blow over

7. When I see a conflict developing which is more important to my partner than to me, I usually:

❑ (a) Express my concerns

❑ (b) Try to help him or her

❑ (c) Let him or her play it out

❑ (d) Leave him or her alone

8. My partner tells me I:

❑ (a) Most times, try to get my own way

❑ (b) Try to work out our conflicts

❑ (c) Am too reasonable, hardly ever get angry

❑ (d) Avoid conflict as much as possible

9. When we are into heavy conflict, I usually:

❑ (a) Talk fast, loud, and hard to make my point

❑ (b) Talk a little more than I listen

❑ (c) Make sure I understand the issue

❑ (d) Try to avoid getting involved

10. When I get angry at my partner I most often:

❑ (a) Raise my voice, start to fight about my point of view

❑ (b) Listen to his or her points, then convince my partner that he or she is wrong

❑ (c) Stay calm while explaining my point of view

❑ (d) Avoid the conflict, tell myself it doesn't really matter

ANALYSIS

When you have completed the assessment, add up how many times you chose a,b,c, or d. Which letter did you choose most? Consider these approaches to conflict.

(a)Aggressive/Controlling

You feel best when you can direct and control your partner. You will likely do what is necessary to gain control over him or her. In heavy conflicts you tend to be intimidating, loud, and judgmental. You are generally contemptuous of your partner if he or she does not stand up for himself or herself. You tend to "lose it" when you feel you are not understood. Your partner is likely afraid of you. You can't really get along with anybody very well. Although you are not likely to admit it, you feel isolated and lonely. Read this chapter again very carefully.

(b) Reasonable/Willful

If you picked mostly "b's," you tend to use your quick mind to deal with conflict with your partner. You are strong willed, ambitious, but not necessarily overbearing. You appeal to reason, rather than brute force when in conflict. You most often are willing to compromise to end long-standing arguments. You will not easily get along with an "a," tend to discount "d's," and feel superior to "c's." Read the anger section carefully.

(c) Rational/Controlled

You don't get fired up very often and will look on in amazement at someone who easily "gets hot under the collar." You listen to your partner's point of view, figure out what's right and wrong about it, then rationally tell him or her what needs to be done to resolve the situation. Having stated your case you tend to defer to your partner in the interest of harmony. You feel most comfortable with a "b," bored with a "d," and try your best to avoid "c's." You appear to handle conflict well, but you need more passion in your life. Read chapter 8 and do all the activities with your partner, without talking too much about them.

(d) Avoiding/Distracting

Picking mostly "d's" indicates that you will probably avoid conflict and open displays of anger at all costs. You likely hold in your feelings, strong as they may be, to keep the peace. You cannot have a strong, passionate, intimate relationship without some openly expressed, then resolved, conflict and anger. "D's" are often paired up with "a's," which is a prescription for misery. You must learn to overcome your fears and deal with the inevitable conflicts that occur in any relationship. Read this chapter carefully again and put what you learn into practice.

Note: No one style of conflict management is, in itself, better than another. Learning how to effectively handle conflict in an intimate relationship means knowing when and how to use all four types, depending on the situation. A bonus is that when you learn how to deal with conflicts and anger in an intimate relationship, handling them in the workplace becomes child's play.

8
SEX IN LONG-TERM RELATIONSHIPS

Laura walked into the bedroom just ahead of Zane. They had just returned from dinner at one of their favorite restaurants. They had spent most of the evening catching up with each other's lives although they had seen each other just that morning. In fact, they saw each other almost every day, except for the usual business trips, since they had been married for 11 years. It had been a fun, romantic evening.

Laura: I was standing facing the mirror when he walked into the bedroom. He gently slid his arm around my body and slowly swung me around toward him. It may sound silly, but it was like a scene from one of those old romantic movies. He cradled my face in his hands and kissed me ever so lightly; his lips brushed mine like a feather. I could feel my body quivering with excited anticipation. I'm telling you it was pure Harlequin romance all the way. He ran his fingertips through the edges of my hair. You can say what you want about your scalp being an erogenous zone, but it sure was for me that night. I wanted him to say, "Let's get out of our clothes," but I was speechless. Instead, and to my delight, he began to very slowly sculpt my shoulders, arms, waist, and back ever so lightly with his fingertips. It was like a first date, you know, tentative yet inviting. Then, if you can imagine after 11 years of marriage, I even got goose bumps as he ran his

fingers slowly up and down my spine. He was a handsome, tall stranger I had fallen passionately in love with. His hands were something else as they slowly caressed my back, then up the outside of my thighs. He didn't touch my breasts — not yet, although by then I wanted it more than anything. I wished our clothes were off, I wanted to be touched all over, to be next to him.

Zane: She was looking at me magnetically as if she wanted flesh to flesh, mouth to mouth, palms to palms, body to body. I was startled as she began rubbing her whole body against mine in animal-like luxuriance, simply enjoying the friction. By some miracle we were still standing, my legs were quivering as she leaned herself against the wall, while at the same time drawing me closer into her. Her hot, moist, now softened lips pressed firmly around my mouth as if she were molding it. She then moved on to my eyes, my nose, while at the same time caressing the shape of my skull, shoulders, and chest. As I relaxed into my near-panic excitement, she suddenly pressed her fingertips deep into my flesh as if she was trying to make the moment more real. My pain smacked more life into my body and increased her frenzied excitement. A speckle of doubt about whether this was my wife or some nameless stranger raced through my mind. I daren't look in case I might break the spell.

Laura: Know what he did next? He began to unzip my dress. I could hardly believe it! Never in a million years did I think having my zipper pulled down would raise such arousal in me — but it did! It must have taken him 15 minutes to coax that zipper down to my hips. I was so aroused, it felt like with each inch someone was turning up the heat so that by the time he finished with it the insides of my thighs were quivering with arousal. But it didn't stop there! He undressed me button by button, inch by inch, the way every woman deserves to be undressed at least once before she dies. I was in such a delirious fog I barely noticed that he began to do what you'd expect him to do to excite me. But by then it didn't matter or it added fuel to the fire; I'm not sure what because I was so hot I could have taken him over and over until we both were exhausted.

Zane: I can hardly remember the details now because it was like our bodies were discovering each other for the first time. It was like I was drugged on the sensations of our flesh touching, our mouths inviting, until our movements became slow and dream like. She began to slowly unbutton my shirt to my waist, my belt, my zipper. Somehow we made it to the bed and without looking she took me to her while she was on her back, then pulled me into her so I could touch the very bottom of her womb, feel its walls again and again. Every cell in my body was awakened to its aliveness as if

some mad man was cranking up the current of some unknown source of energy. A spring-like tension drove tightness through my entire body until I surrendered every muscle, pore, cell, or remains of willpower.

Laura: Never had I experienced such confusing pleasure. I vaguely remember crying out something, then a blurted sob and most surprisingly a giggle as joy rippled through my body. Mother would never approve.

Zane: My body shuddered. I slipped into surrender's downy quilt, faded, then died as we gently lay together in an all-encompassing embrace. A soothing familiar wave flowed through my entire being. We gazed at each other, not wanting to say anything that might break the spell. As I looked into her familiar, loving eyes, tears of joy streamed down my face in appreciation of our love and closeness. It was amazing to feel this after 11 years of marriage, two kids, and a house.

Just down the street Drew and Sandy Davis had finished the evening's silent ritual of watching the late news, putting out the cat, checking the doors, programming the coffee maker, brushing their teeth, and finally arriving in bed separately at 11:55 p.m. Drew sets the alarm for 6:23 a.m. A perfunctory kiss "goodnight dear" sends them off to the opposite sides of the queen-sized bed — a king-sized gulf of loneliness between them. Lying on their sides, their backs to each other, eyes agaze in the comfort of the dark silence, their muttering minds carry on a private, resentful conversation about one of their many ongoing conflicts accumulated during their eight-year marriage.

Drew: I'm so horny it hurts. But of course *she's* not interested —

she never is. If I approach her now she'll probably say it's too late. If I don't get some soon I'm going to explode. I'm not even sure I want to do it with her anyway.

Sandy: Oh god, here we go. I can always tell when he's hot to trot. His comment about the woman in the news, a late-night shower, a few grabs and remarks throughout the evening, not so subtle moans and groans, his hot body. The Big Signals; he's so predictable. He doesn't really care about *me,* he's just interested in getting his rocks off. If he treated me like a woman he loved and cared about, I might be a little more amenable when we go to bed. What does he think I am? A machine?

Drew: I could slide over and kiss her but what's the use? She's about as enthusiastic as a dead chicken. God, I'm hot. (He squirms, moans, and stretches out to touch her.) Maybe I could make believe she's Donna at the office. What a hot number that one is. Umm. (He reaches over and begins to rub her neck.)

Sandy: Oh no, here it comes, the Big Move. Maybe if I pretended I'm sleeping he'll go away.

Drew: She's doing the old dead-as-a-doornail number. I'd be better off with one of those blow-up dolls.

Sandy: He's not stopping, maybe I should just give in and get it over with. It's only a matter of a few minutes. Damn, that's even too long, once we start he'll be all over me, it'll hurt like it always does. He'll go off, I'll be a mess. I'll have to get up to go to the bathroom, while he rolls over and goes to sleep. Ugh.

Drew: I'm so hot but if I go through with it now, I just know I'll come too fast. No wonder — trying to make love to her is so degrading she makes me feel like she's doing me some sort of favor — no response at all. I'm going to hate myself after, I just know it. But I'm so hot now!

Sandy: This is great! Like two dogs in the street. What's happened? I used to enjoy sex, even with Drew at the beginning. God, I feel awful.

Drew: Oh here it comes the great angry-dead submission. Why not go ahead, I deserve it. I can't help it if she's frigid, I need my sex even if she doesn't. (He rolls over; she motionlessly submits and he comes almost instantly. He rolls off her in some relief but is also filled with self-hatred.) What's happening to me? I can't even turn on my wife or enjoy sex anymore, what's the use?

(By the time Sandy returns from the bathroom, Drew is sleeping on his side of the bed. She gives him a resentful glance then slips under the covers, resigned to the fact that it will take an hour or so before the hurt leaves the pit of her stomach and she slips into the relief of sleep.)

Those scenes represent the polar opposites; from what is possible to what is all too common in long-term relationships. Each is as insidious as the other. Laura and Zane's serendipitous encounter, or our own personalized facsimile, is the kind of experience we long for or are told is the goal of sex in relationships. Drew and Sandy's painful, reluctant mechanics are what many couples resign themselves to rather than face the fact that their relationship is in trouble. Their so-called sexual difficulties are merely symptoms of the deeper issues in their marriage.

As you read the above scenes, what were your reactions?

I felt angered by _____

_____

I felt delighted by _____

_____

I felt embarrassed by _____

_____

I was disgusted by _____

_____

My body reactions were _____

_____

What judgments were you making about the scenes? (Were they realistic, immoral, not graphic enough?) _____

_____

What parts would men like and dislike? _____

_____

What sections would be titillating or a turn-off to women? _____

_____

Did any vivid images pop into your mind? _____

_____

What parts can you *not* now remember? _____

_____

Read the scenes over again. Write down the following phrase —

Sex is... _____

_____

_____

_____

and complete it with whatever comes to your mind, as many times as you can.

Think about when, how, where, and why you developed your attitudes toward sex. Which attitudes inhibit your sexual behavior? Which are your freeing attitudes?

a. THE CIVILIZATION OF SEX

Women and men everywhere have always been and will continue to be preoccupied with and insecure about their sexuality. The womb and the phallus have been both worshipped and degraded by civilized societies. Most ancient cultures produced some kind of do-it-yourself sex manual complete with graphic illustrations. *The Joy of Sex; A Cordon Bleu Guide to Lovemaking*, and Dr. Ruth Westheimer's TV program "Good Sex," are simply contemporary versions of that ancient tradition. Civilizations, especially those which have sophisticated bureaucracies, have demanded that men and women repress their sexuality in order to produce the goods and services necessary for the continuance of society. The family, church, educational system, and private industry have participated in co-opting people's natural sexuality. This has been done in the form of various rewards and punishments, depending on the particular institution.

Each of us can vividly recall from our childhood some incident or cruel phrase that was designed to thwart our blossoming curiosity about the newly discovered sensations rising up from our loins that made us blind with excitement. Because most people do not understand or appreciate that sexual repression is part of living in a civilized society, a cure is sought for "sexual problems" as if those problems were like a wart that needed to be removed. Each of us is, in one way or another, sexually repressed, which means that we will have difficulties experiencing sexual pleasure. If you want more sexual pleasure in your primary, loving, intimate relationship it means countering the norms of society plus most of what you were taught from the day you were born. It means, for example, adopting at least some of the following attitudes: sex can be fun; sex is only one small part of relationship; working hard decreases your sexual pleasure; women are equal to men; to get what you want you have to ask directly and specifically for what you want; sex need not be pleasurable or exciting for both partners at the same time; sexual encounters need to be planned most of the time; sexual fantasies are part of being human, they don't have to be acted out; it can be pleasurable to have sex with a partner who is not interested, as long as he or she agrees to it.

There is no longer any such thing as "natural sexuality." We have been civilized to the point that our natural sexuality has been lost forever. It's like New York's original natural environment; it has been so altered that it doesn't really exist anymore. Although the rivers still flow, the ocean influences the city, the weather patterns still persist, they are radically different than they were in their natural form; they are now "urbanized." The same is true of our sexuality; it has been "civilized." Some of our basic biological urges still remain but they must be considered within our cultural context. For example, a man is sexually attracted to a woman. A minuscule part of that attraction is because he is a male responding biologically to her femaleness; the rest is a result of his living in a particular city, in a certain kind of neighborhood, his relationship with his mother and father, his future aspirations, etc. His desire for a particular kind of woman with a specific body type or color of hair will also be influenced by the kinds of magazines, books, and television programs he was brought up on. Whether the woman is attracted to him will be influenced by a reciprocal set of factors. Neither of them is aware of those influences and each thinks that "it's natural." The kinds of people you are attracted to tell you a lot about how you have been socialized, what your values are, your aspirations, and the kind of environment you came from.

Create a profile of the kind of man or woman to whom you are most attracted. Describe him or her in specific detail.

His/her body (without clothes) is _____

_____

_____

He or she wears_____

_____

_____

He or she works at _____

_____

He or she would think this way _____

_____

_____

He or she would say the following things to me in particular circumstances _____

_____

_____

_____

If you need help doing this, go to a shopping mall and observe the people there. Make a list of what you're attracted to and what you're not. Continue the process until you've created a profile of the ideal person.

The next step is to think about what this profile reveals of *you*. Write that down.

_____

_____

_____

_____

_____

_____

_____

_____

_____

b. BASIC OPERATING ASSUMPTIONS

Before we go any further we would like to state some of our basic operating assumptions and biases about sex and sex therapy. They are implied in what we write, but we want to make them explicit because in our experience, whenever we talk about this topic people distort what we say because of their own morality. Also, everything in this chapter applies only to "normal, neurotic" heterosexual couples, both of whom willingly choose to engage in sex whether they like it or not.

(a) When it comes to sex, we are all more or less neurotic. If we could accept this fact, our lives would be more pleasurable.

(b) Almost everything we learn about what it takes and what it means to be successful in this society guarantees sexual dissatisfaction.

(c) Most sex therapies operate on the assumption that if you learn to do everything "right," then you'll have a good sex life. Our assumption is that not every symptom can or should be fixed. You may be better off to accept yourself as you are while you discover interesting and creative ways of living with your present limitations.

(d) Sex is not a basic human need. The need for sex indicates your inability to deal with your individuality, i.e., your aloneness.

(e) A sexual problem exists whenever you say so; it is not just in your head. Most sexual problems don't exist in a vacuum; they are indications of how you relate to yourself and to the world.

(f) Nobody can turn you on or off, you turn yourself on or off over a person and what they do or do not do. Nobody can give you pleasure, you please yourself over what the other does.

(g) You are not as interested in sex as you say or think you are. Your obsession with sex is a defense against dealing with yourself.

(h) The male experience of sex and the female experience of sex is like night and day. It is impossible for a man to completely understand a woman's sexual experience and vice versa. That can open up a lifetime of interesting adventures and conversations.

(i) The Sexual Revolution may have altered your mind, however, it has not yet descended into your genitals.

(j) Research about sex is, at best, of marginal value. What is needed is to teach people how to create a personalized philosophy about their sexuality.

(k) While everything you are as a woman or man is expressed in your sexual relationship, sex is not essential to producing a loving, intimate life together.

(l) Sex for most couples has more to do with power and control than love or intimacy.

(m) Sex in brief or early romantic encounters is a completely different experience than sex in long-term relationships. The former is touted to be the ideal, the latter is what we all secretly long for.

(n) Sexual excitement and sexual pleasure are mutually exclusive.

We think that your sexual behavior and feelings are governed by the assumptions you make about sex. You are probably living by a set of assumptions that you learned as a child but that are now out of date. By becoming familiar with those assumptions you will be in a better position to be more satisfied with yourself sexually.

c. SEX IS NOT A FOUR-LETTER WORD

Sex usually conjures up at least two four-letter words: love; and the expletive for

Take out a piece of paper and begin writing down your assumptions about sex. Add to your list as you read through this chapter. Put an "X" beside those assumptions you would like to change and a "+" beside those you feel good about.

Rewrite the assumptions you would like to change in a way that would more closely reflect how you *currently* would like to think about sex and your experience of it. What behaviors must you alter to bring about this change?

Talk with your partner about what behaviors you would like your partner to change. Try out one new behavior the next time you have sex together.

intercourse, fuck. In common conversation, women are more likely to associate sex with love. Loving is associated with the warm, friendly, soft, relaxed, intimate, receptive, sensual, passive, and relational qualities women are taught to value and pursue. The word fuck conjures up images of aggressiveness, hardness, being goal-oriented, the impersonal, domination, penetration, the lurid, the perverse — all of which are aspects of the male stereotype.

The feminine and masculine exist along a continuum. Each of us has aspects of both, each of us tends more toward one end of the scale than the other. Your sexual self-image is an indication of how comfortable you are with your position.

Look at the continuum line in Figure #9. Put an "X" where you see yourself. Write an "L" where you would like to be. Put a "P" where you think your partner is on the scale. Talk together about your individual assessments.

d. SEXUAL PROBLEMS

It seems only logical that people would have an interest in exploring, watching, and understanding this thing called sex. By a glance, or a brush of your hands, sex can produce a flood of uncontrollable, delightful, scary sensations that can make you lose touch with all reason and rationality.

It is also logical that so many sexual problems exist, given how many "bad"

FIGURE #9

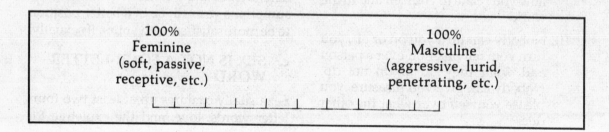

messages we were given in our childhood about our bodies. Added to this are the confusing messages we receive in our adult life about what good sex is. Most of us have fertile minds and uptight bodies in which problems can flourish and grow.

We all have sexual problems of one sort or another depending on the circumstances of our life and who we are with. Sexual problems fall into one or more of three categories: functional disabilities; questions about the appropriateness of certain sexual urges; wanting more satisfaction in the sexual encounter. (Note, we are referring to sex between consenting adults who are in a long-term relationship.)

Functional disabilities can fit into two classes: organic and intrapersonal. If you suspect that you have an organically caused functional problem, you should have a complete medical checkup by a specialist who has extensive experience in treating sexual dysfunctions and who is open to accepting other than organic causes of the problem. We recommend that women be treated by a woman since female physicians are likely to be more understanding of how a woman's body and mind function. It is crucial that the physician, female or male, be empathetic and willing to listen to your fears. If you feel that you're not getting a sympathetic response, go to another physician. Moralistic or harsh treatment by any professional will only create new problems. Don't stand for it, under any circumstances.

If your dysfunction is diagnosed as not being organic, it's time for introspection, self-disclosure, and risk taking. The most common intrapersonal sexual dysfunctions of the male are impotence, premature ejaculation, and retarded ejaculation. The most common intrapersonal sexual dysfunctions of the female are general sexual dysfunction (so-called frigidity), difficulty in reaching orgasm, and pain during intercourse. These sexual problems are intrapersonal because the main source of the difficulty usually lies in the individual's inability or unwillingness to disclose fears, inadequacies, conflicts, or lack of knowledge about sex. The result is that the sexual experience for both partners becomes distasteful or conflicted. *These problems do not lend themselves to the self-help approach because the causes are multiple and interrelated.* If you have any of these problems, find yourselves a good counselor. Chapter 9 gives you some tips on how to do that.

The other two kinds of "sexual problems" — questions about the appropriateness of your sexual urges and wanting more sexual pleasure and intimacy in your long-term relationship — can be explored using self-help methods.

Our approach to couples' sexual concerns is an educational one. We don't just treat the specific sexual problems, but help you find creative ways of addressing painful feelings. Ignorance, fear, shame, and anxiety feed on themselves. Our first goal is to help you understand that these feelings are normal responses to intimate sexual relations, but with disclosing and exploring those feelings with your partner, ignorance can be transformed into confident self-awareness, fear into excitement, shame into self-acceptance, and anxiety into joyful pleasure. Our assumption is that couples can, through self-examination and experimentation, define what is good sex for them in their particular situation. This is what we refer to as the creative, artistic approach to sex. It means that both people are willing to courageously face whatever comes up in the exploration. It assumes you have acquired, and are continuing to acquire, the skills outlined in the previous chapters. We also assume you're interested in living a creative life, in all its dimensions.

Answer true or false

_____ 1. Sometimes I pretend to be interested in sex when really I'm not interested.

_____ 2. I think I respond too slowly.

_____ 3. I think my partner sees me as too slow.

_____ 4. I respond too quickly with my partner.

_____ 5. Sometimes I fake orgasms.

_____ 6. I feel disappointed if I don't have an orgasm at the same time as my partner.

_____ 7. I think my partner fakes orgasm.

_____ 8. I think my partner pretends to be interested in me sexually.

_____ 9. Sometimes I make up excuses to avoid sex. My favorite excuse is....

_____ 10. I know I have a sexual problem but I don't want to talk about it.

_____ 11. I think I should have an orgasm to please my partner.

_____ 12. I don't tell my partner when he or she is hurting me.

_____ 13. I think my partner has problems but I don't talk about it.

_____ 14. I feel good about myself sexually.

Share your answers with your partner only if he or she has completed this assessment and is willing to read this entire chapter.

e. INTIMACY OR SEXUAL EXCITEMENT: SEX THROUGH THE SIX STAGES

Human beings are not by nature sexual; but we choose to be so. You cannot live very long without air or water, but you can live happily to a ripe old age without sex. The role sex plays in your life, the importance you give to it, your attitudes toward your sexual urges, and your behavioral responses to sexual arousal are all a matter of free choice.

There are four fundamental elements in your relationship: sex (satisfaction versus dissatisfaction); love (do you love, and are you loved); marriage (whether to marry or not); and children (to have or not to have). Each of these four elements exists independently. For example, love can exist without sex, sex can be enjoyed without love, a marriage can function happily without sex, children can be born and raised outside the institution of marriage. Relationships usually begin with two people falling in love. Sexual excitement accompanies and is associated with the thrill of falling in love. Because of this coincidence, love and sexual excitement are assumed to be connected, but in fact they are not. This erroneous connection is very dangerous and has destroyed countless marriages, dismembered families, and disrupted promising and otherwise meaningful relationships. Many people attribute their dissatisfaction with life in terms of sexual problems, but their real difficulty is misunderstanding the role of intimacy and sex in a relationship. They feel that the excitement of the first romantic encounter is "it," when in fact the sexual experience in long-term relationships is constantly developing and changing; it is as free as a bird. It is only when you imprison it in a cage of romantic fantasies that it becomes docile, sluggish, or even perverted. That simple insight, if you integrate it into your life, can liberate you from your self-imposed pain of frustrating or boring sex.

In our experience working with couples, it has become clear that a couple's sexual development changes as they go through the six stages of relationship. Most people do not appreciate that their sexual relationship will change as a result of their interpersonal dynamics.

1. The romantic stage

During the romantic stage of falling in love, a couple's sexual feelings toward one another are readily available to them. They experience a lot of sexual feelings; they feel open to each other; they are able to enjoy one another sexually. There is a sense of excitement and novelty during this time. Much of the enjoyment of this stage is generated by the fact that they don't know each other well; each is putting his or her best foot forward. If they (usually it's she) decide "not to go all the way" until they are married or ready to make some other kind of commitment, the excitement will be increased as the anticipation grows.

2. The early commitment stage

If a couple is having a good time sexually, they will begin to explore the second stage of relationship. They might come to the conclusion that they should make some kind of commitment by either getting married or moving in together. Once they do that their sexual excitement will begin to drop off because in the day-to-day closeness of living together the freshness begins to wear off. The basic ingredients of sexual excitement in the first blush of meeting are newness and mystery. Anything new is exciting. When you make an early commitment some of the mystery is lost. When

ACTIVITY #39
SEXUAL FANTASIES

What are your romantic sexual fantasies? (If you do not wish to write them in full, at least write down a key word that reminds you of the fantasy.)

Do you expect sex to have meaning (rather than pleasure)? _____

For you, does sex have meaning only in connection with love? _____

For you, can sex without love give pleasure like a bag of salty peanuts hurriedly gobbled? _____

What, to you, is ideal sex? _____

What are your attitudes toward sexual techniques? _____

Do you dream of lifelong sexual excitement with your partner? _____

What do you think is necessary to make this dream come true? _____

you're living together it is much more difficult to maintain the image of the perfect partner as you see him or her drag out of bed in the morning or share the daily toilette. These events speed you with alarming vigor into the third stage, the inevitable conflict/power struggles.

3. The conflict/power struggle stage

The conflict/power struggle stage is the crucial turning point for most couples' sexual experience. As their disagreements and difficulties arise, their feelings about one another will change. There will be times when they don't like each other much. The images begin to crumble during the arguments as each person tries to win. Sexual excitement fades away as more of the newness and mystery is lost in the struggle.

Because your partner is not living up to your romantic image you become angry and disappointed. You then begin to find faults in your partner, or you might become bored with your sexual relationship. One or both of you may withdraw emotionally. Often one partner will withhold sex while the other relentlessly and resentfully pursues it, which is another symptom of the power struggle.

Some couples fight, then have great sex together. Others can't have sex until they've had a fight, which is a sign of their unhealthy dependence on each other and an indication that they fear intimacy. In their fights they emotionally push each other to a distance where it is safe enough for them to have sex. It's like having sex with a stranger — very physical but no intimacy or commitment. If these things go on for a long time, you will move to the next stage of resignation.

4. The resignation or reality stage

In the resignation stage you make the statement, "This is the best I can hope for." You decide that your relationship is not going to get much better. You give up and resign yourself to the battle of the sexes. Your arguments go around in circles. You may cycle back to the romantic stage when you feel a bit of the spark again, perhaps while you're on vacation or during some other exciting event that brings some promise, but in the long run you notice that you're in a pattern of relating in which your sexual encounters are less frequent, predictable, and uninteresting. There is, however, another possibility.

If you are willing and able to resolve your conflicts and power struggles, you can move on to the reality stage. In this stage you look at your own sexuality as well as examine how you relate together sexually. *You begin to do something about your sexual relationship.*

The first step is to accept yourself as you are, and accept your partner as he or she is; you take responsibility for yourself in your relationship. When you do that you set the scene for the next stage, which is commitment. Activity #40 will help you move into the next stage.

By bringing these feelings and attitudes to the surface you will have a chance to integrate them into your life, and to prevent them from being stumbling blocks to the kind of sexuality you would like. By sharing each other's story at this stage, you will become more empathetic, more open, more available to each other, which can result in deeper sexual intimacy.

5. The full commitment stage

By working through your conflicts and power struggles, and by seeing each other as you really are, you move on to the full commitment stage. At this stage you can say, "Look, I think it's possible to explore more of my sexuality and sexual pleasure with you. I'm willing to risk doing that with you. Are you interested?" If two people can make that commitment to themselves and each other, they are ready to move on to the next stage.

Each of us brings our unique experiences to our sexual encounters. This uniqueness is developed out of our personal histories. Our life stories are created out of our own perspectives as men or women in this society, plus our own definitions of our sexual identity. One way of discovering more about your sexual self is to write out your sexual history. It usually takes five or six hours over a period of four to five days to do this. Allow yourself time to think about events and your reactions to those events. Include things like how sex was viewed in your family, what you were taught about sex, remembrances of your initial sexual awakenings, when you first started masturbating or looking in the medical books in your house. Include what your mother or father told you about sex, if anything. What were your impressions of your parents' sexual relationship. Can you remember your first sexual encounter? Was it enjoyable, frightening, or disappointing? Include the sexual history of your present relationship. Write down your thoughts about who you are as a sexual being including your hopes and dreams about your sexual experience. The first time you do this may be difficult, even frightening. If you feel it necessary, talk to a trusted friend or counselor about your experiences as you write this. When you've finished, share your history with your partner. Have your partner read your history out loud to you and vice versa.

Relate your history to your partner in three different ways: as a tragedy, as a success story, and as a hilarious comedy.

6.   The mature romance stage

The sixth stage, mature romance, means that you are willing to disclose yourself to each other. You begin to explore your likes and dislikes, your areas of fear and sensitivity. You agree to talk openly about the difficulties and pleasures that you may be experiencing sexually. As you do this your emotional connection develops and you allow yourselves to be completely vulnerable with each other much like you were in the romantic stage, only this time you are doing it with your eyes open. In mature romance you feel emotionally, physically, and spiritually understood by your partner. You create a sense of unity with one another, and out of this unity you make your dreams come true.

In moving from the romantic stage to the mature romance stage, your sexual relating takes on a different feeling. At the romantic stage, the statement is, "I *need* you and I *must* be with you to experience my sexual excitement." There is an urgency that shoots through your entire body. The two of you are really turned on to each other. In mature romance you have a different kind of sexual experience; it is a slower deep body pleasure combined with an emotional depth created out of your shared history together. In mature romance, you say, "I *want* to be with you." During the sexual experience there is a feeling of joining two worlds — the feeling of, "I have been touched, I am understood, and I can let go." We believe these feelings fill a deep profound human need within each of us, and the sexual relationship is one way of experiencing those feelings.

The rest of this chapter is based on the assumption that you have at least reached the reality stage and are willing to risk exploring your sexuality together. We also assume that when you have disagreements you will remember to use the skills you learned in the chapters on communications, conflict, and anger.

f. EXCITE YOUR MIND — PLEASE YOUR BODY

There are two fundamental sources of your sexual experience: your mind and your body. It is in your mind that you create your expectations of sex and your dreams about how it should be or might be. Your mind creates sexual excitement; sexual pleasure arises out of being aware of and in contact with your body.

1. Your mind

Your sexual attractions and fantasies are generated within the confines of your mind. What goes on in your mind certainly affects your body, as anyone who has felt that shiver of excitement upon seeing Mr. or Ms. Wonderful across the room will testify. It is in your mind that you manufacture sexual excitement — that frightening ecstatic emotion that sends jolts of energy into your loins, makes your legs quiver, your stomach queasy, your mouth babble, and that can make you forget all your cares and woes. As mentioned before, this reaction happens at the romantic stage of relationship. It is a psychophysiological chain reaction that goes something like this: you see someone you're attracted to; the awareness of this attraction triggers off unconscious questions such as, "Can I get him interested in me?" "Who is this mysterious person?" "What a challenge, what do I have to do to get her in my grasp?"; your mind sends messages to your body to prepare for the chase; your body reacts — your eyes open wide, your heart beats rapidly; your mind sends signals to your body to produce the necessary biochemical reactions to either go after him or her or run away from the situation. These reactions and the accompanying physical sensations — excitement in your stomach, blurred vision, unclear thoughts, hot loins and slurred speech — is like going over the downward side of a ferris wheel. You feel queasy and you scream with both fear and delight because for a brief instant you don't know what will happen.

Within this context it is easy to understand why sexual excitement fades away in long-term relationships. The mystery and chase are over; the ferris wheel ride is finished.

2. Your body

The other source of your sexual experience is your body. It is through your body that you become aware of sexual pleasure. The pleasure emanates from your willingness and ability to allow prolonged body contact. Sexual pleasure is very different from sexual excitement. A prerequisite for sexual pleasure in long-term relationships is vulnerability, intimacy, and a relaxed mind. Sexual excitement is contingent upon control, mystery, and a busy mind. Sexual pleasure is a result of being willing to give in to the irrational; sexual excitement is an attempt to overcome your sense of helplessness by gaining control over the other.

Body contact is an important source of pleasure. Skin is potentially a huge pleasure or pain receptor. Basking in the warmth of a loving embrace attests to the good feelings that are possible through body contact, just as the unwanted touch of a stranger can send a painful chill into your heart.

We all hunger for body contact and the comfort it can bring. If unfulfilled, it can have serious emotional consequences. Studies have shown that young children when left untouched die at a much higher rate than children who, in a similar state of

Think about the last time you were sexually excited by someone. What were your body reactions? Where in your body did you feel it the most? What thoughts go through your mind when you become sexually excited? Or does your mind go blank? Do you move toward or avoid people to whom you are sexually attracted? If you are in a primary, committed relationship, what assumptions do you make about being sexually attracted to another person?

health, are held and caressed. The more advanced hospitals are incorporating this into their programs on children's wards by encouraging parents to physically comfort their sick children.

We live in a society in which touching is either discouraged or perverted. Mouthwash commercials tell us of disgusting germs and odors in our mouths. Soap commercials show people scrubbing away body odors. The latest feminine hygiene sprays zap any errant natural smell out of existence so that sexual areas are "clean and inviting." Many couples have one leg out of the bed almost before they finish lovemaking so they can wash away the sweat and those undesirable body fluids. When we see two men warmly embracing, thoughts of homosexuality immediately spring to our minds. Even when touching is allowed between men and women thoughts of sexual performance have to be taken into account.

So, in touching, we have to be concerned with how much is too much, or how long is too long, before our actions are misinterpreted. These difficulties with touching have been highlighted by increased incidence of child sexual abuse, sexual harassment in the workplace, and the fear of catching a sexually transmitted disease.

In long-term relationships the lack of body contact, both non-sexual and sexual, is a *symptom* of problems, not the problem itself. When two people are maintaining clear communication and are keeping up to date on their appreciations, resentments, and emotions they will feel like touching each other and will feel good about their partner touching them. However, we all carry some shame about our bodies as a result of growing up in this society. In your sexual relationship you can explore your shame together so that you can become more comfortable with your body. The more you are aware of your body and the more you can accept it, the deeper will you be able to experience sexual pleasure.

3. Exploring your sexual fantasies

We think that too much emphasis is placed on sexual excitement in this society. Popular music, soap operas, romance novels, and popular "men's" and "women's" magazines all portray and imply that unless you have bell-ringing, toe-tingling sex, something is wrong. In our view these attitudes can only lead to a sense of failure, self-deception, dissatisfaction, and resignation for those people who choose to be in long-term relationships. Once you've lived through and resolved the conflicts and power struggles you can never return to the excitement you felt in those moments or months after you first met. It's like trying to relive the past; it can't be done. Cherish the memory and move on to the present.

It is possible, however, to experience interest, fun, love, creativity, even sexual excitement tempered by your history together. One way of doing this is by exploring and sharing your fantasies together. Sexual fantasies are part of the human experience and are a way of discovering more about yourselves. Fantasies allow you to expand your reality, make it larger than life, and get in touch with your spirituality. Sharing sexual fantasies can be a creative way of communicating and deepening intimacy. Five rules must be followed for this to occur:

(a) Both partners must agree that they have reached at least the commitment stage of relationship and have the skills and goodwill necessary to deal with the misunderstandings and difficulties that may arise as a result of sharing your fantasies. You agree that if you get into trouble you will consult a counselor immediately.

(b) Both partners agree to share verbally all the sexual fantasies that you have when you are together as well as when you are not together.

(c) You both agree to respect the other's right to enjoy, dislike, or not participate in the other's fantasies. You both also acknowledge that women's and men's fantasies are different and often don't interest the other.

(d) Each of you clearly understands that sharing a sexual fantasy does not necessarily mean that it must or will be acted out.

(e) Any feelings of jealousy, rejection, hurt, or anger that arise out of a partner's fantasy will be acknowledged as legitimate feelings and will be grounds for examining one's self, rather than punishing the partner for having the fantasy.

Normal, healthy, creative women and men can entertain themselves in the exhilaration of sexual fantasies. They explore them, accept them, take pleasure in them, and learn from them. It's like going to a play or movie, which in essence is the writer's fantasies brought to life on the stage or screen. You may choose to live out some of your fantasies, but would never consider acting out others. Some fantasies are exciting just to imagine; that in itself is enough. Since they are arousing, they can lead to more exciting sex with your partner.

Our rigid, puritanical society often condemns sexual fantasies as perverted, sick, bad, immoral, or wrong. There is a fear that you will be taken over by the fantasies. This is not true for the average person, and if shared within the confines of a loving, long-term relationship you'll actually lose interest in your current fantasies, just as you would become bored after watching your favorite movie five or six times.

4. Staying in contact

In long-term relationships, your sexual encounters will not always be exciting or pleasurable. Many times you will find yourself having sex and discover that it's mundane or boring. That's okay. Boring sex does not diminish the presence of love. In fact, boring sex can be a source of humor and intimacy for both of you, if you can share your boredom in a lighthearted way. Being bored can actually be quite relaxing and may open up the possibility for just experiencing the pleasure of having intimate, physical body contact. It can be a rough world out there, sometimes all we need to recover from it is a warm, loving person to cuddle up with.

The following activities are ways of sustaining intimate contact without sexual activity.

This activity is best done in front of a full-length mirror. We recommend that you have one in your bedroom. It can easily be affixed to any wall. Use it to get to know your body.

Stand in front of the mirror and begin to slowly take off your clothes. If you are feeling comfortable enough, have your partner take off your clothes. Make an agreement not to seduce each other during this activity. Acknowledge it, if you become aroused, but do not act on it. By making this agreement you will feel freer to explore your body without the pressure of having sex. Also, you might want to start moving toward intercourse just at the point when you're becoming embarrassed or frightened. Breathe and stay with the exploration if you can. However, you can stop at any time you wish; *you* decide what you can handle.

Put on some soft, relaxing music if you wish. Make sure the room is warm and that you are not going to be disturbed. Lock the door. Take the phone off the hook. Don't use alcohol or other drugs while doing this activity.

Once you have removed your clothes begin to explore your body. Take a look at your feet, look for signs of care and age. Feel your feet. Explore your legs, the muscles in your legs, check out the shape and detail of your knees. Then move slowly up to your thighs and hips. Examine your pubic hair. Is it curly, sparse, dark or light? Take a good look at your genitals — the area of our bodies we were told not to touch or spend too much time with when we were children. If you feel "funny" doing this, breathe, and let yourself giggle. It's all right to be embarrassed or to have fun.

Now take a look at your back. Note any hair, dimples, creases, or stretch marks. Observe the muscles, your shoulder blades, and spinal column. Do you have those famous "love handles" around your waist? Look at your abdomen. Are you plump or thin around your belly? Do you have scars? Is your navel an "innie" or an "outie?"

Take a look at your chest, note the differences from left to right, check the muscles, hair growth, color. How are you feeling about your body? Are you still breathing? Carry on the exploration to your shoulders, arms, hands, neck, and your head.

If you want to take another risk, begin slowly to explore each other's bodies. Remember to keep your agreement not to seduce each other. Allow your feelings; but don't act on them. You may want to lie down on the bed to do this. Talk to each other. Be aware of any feelings of embarrassment about your partner looking at you or you looking at her or him. Ask each other where you experience the most pleasure when you are touched. Ask, or tell each other how to touch the most pleasurable areas. If you want your partner to stop something you don't like make sure you tell him or her. This is not an endurance test. You can determine how far you want to go. It's important that you do so in order to experience a sense of self-responsibility. Each of us has our limits and it is up to us to decide whether we want to extend those limits. Love requires that our partners respect those limits.

Talk together to find out how free you feel with each other. You may feel awkward doing this the first few times but it can be used as a way of developing your capacity for more sexual pleasure together. Sometimes it takes years to open up to each other. Allow yourself time. Go at your own pace. Also recognize that by taking a few risks you will begin to become more aware of yourself. Take some time to write down your experiences.

_____

_____

_____

_____

_____

_____

_____

_____

_____

_____

_____

_____

_____

_____

_____

_____

_____

_____

_____

_____

_____

_____

_____

_____

_____

Take some time alone to think about your current sexual fantasies. See if you can develop one of them in more detail. What do the characters look like? Are they people you know? Where is the setting for your fantasy? How old are you and the players? Close your eyes and let your mind drift to the fantasy a bit more to observe the details. Share this fantasy with your partner. Be aware of your thoughts and feelings as you talk about it with him or her. Talk together about what fantasies you have that you may want to act out. If you agree, try acting one of them out following the five rules outlined in section 3.

(a) Take at least 22 minutes each day to be alone together. Don't allow any disturbances.

(b) Once a week have your partner tickle or lightly stroke your back for about 10 minutes. Return the favor.

(c) Every day make non-sexual physical contact when you get up in the morning, when you part, and when you meet again in the evening.

(d) When you hug be aware of when you become uncomfortable and what you do to break contact in your discomfort.

(e) Go to a professional masseur or masseuse once a week for three weeks.

(f) Spend one evening about every two weeks being in close physical contact, without having intercourse: touch, stroke, embrace, give each other a bath, wash and dry your partner's hair, do a face massage. When you become aroused during these activities just let your sensations be there, don't act on them. This is particularly important for men. If you get an erection during these times, acknowledge that fact and just let it be there.

(g) If you usually wear nightclothes to bed, don't for a week. Allow yourself to freely walk nude in your bedroom with your partner present.

(h) Think of all the things you normally wouldn't ask of your partner. Ask for them, respecting your partner's option to refuse or agree. If he or she agrees, be specific in your instructions. If your partner refuses, watch how you pout and punish.

g. YOUR CEILING MAY BE YOUR PARTNER'S FLOOR

As if we didn't have enough obstacles to satisfying sex between women and men, there are two more that have a profound influence on a couple's sex life.

(a) Women and men do not understand or accept each other sexually. In response, women most often comply or withdraw sexually. Men characteristically attempt to force sex on women, use guilt to manipulate them into it, or withdraw generally.

(b) Often sex therapy and the definition of good sex is male-oriented and reflects the bias in our culture toward the male viewpoint. The concept of what good sex is from the standpoint of women is not very well developed. This presents difficulties for both men and women. Men become frustrated at "not being able to please her," while many women live with a sometimes vague sense of resentment about not being understood sexually by their partners.

The difficulties in achieving understanding between the sexes are compounded by our individual preferences about what is pleasurable and what is not. All of this means that you can't make love to or be satisfied by a statistical average or a social dilemma. You can, however, have pleasurable sex with a particular person. But in order to do so, both of you must be willing to explore your unique likes and dislikes, your peculiarities and discretions. Nothing beats verbal communication when you are attempting to explore your sexuality together. Remember, however, that talking is not enough. She may not be able to tell him ahead of time what she likes and dislikes. Even if she recalls that passionate sensation of him stroking her thighs on their tenth date, she may not be turned on by it any more. Or, if she remembers how a former lover gently caressed her temples while brushing her lips with his, she might discreetly decide that this is not the time to tell her present partner about that. She is going to discover what she likes and what she finds pleasurable at this moment (it may be different next time) by telling him what to do or by taking his hand in hers and placing it where she wants it. She can then let him know more of what turns her on by encouraging him or through more detailed suggestions (i.e., "Please do it a little lighter; oh yes, that's it!"). Transmitted with sensual directness, and within the context of an intimate long-term relationship, these kinds of risks are likely to create excitement.

For his part, he will have to rethink his attitudes toward women and sex. Our experience is that most men assume they have to initiate sex, that sex is something done in bed, that they know what pleases a woman, that they are more sexually sophisticated than women, that ejaculating inside her vagina is what sex is all about, that women are not really interested in sex —they do it as a favor to men, and that new sexual techniques designed to turn her on will get good results. Male chauvinism is alive and well in the male psyche. We consistently hear from women that they do not hate sex; they hate sex only with men who artificially separate love and sexuality. Women tell us that when they are treated as vibrant, worthwhile, valuable, and equal beings, they are willing to open themselves to their male partners sexually and otherwise.

Men, if they can allow it, find physical arousal to be pleasurable. Most men enjoy a firmer, stronger touch than do the majority of women. Men often find that a very light touch is annoying, not arousing. What is gentle, fast, slow, or sensual cannot be put into words. Partners must show each other what is pleasurable. Men have a tendency to hurry sex, to "get down to business," which is a turn-off for most women. If men can learn to slow their pace they will learn to savor the sensory pleasure that can only be experienced by allowing one's body to be completely aroused. Time is of the essence — taking a long time for sexual lovemaking is likely to bring more pleasure, relaxation, and satisfaction.

Our male clients tell us that one of their fears about allowing themselves to be aroused by their partner is that they will "come" while their partner is stimulating them. Men seem to assume that they have to hang on to their ejaculation like a little kid who has to go to the bathroom halfway home from school and is afraid of going in his pants. The pain is excruciating. In talking to women it seems that when they were enjoying arousing their partners and when they felt love and intimacy were part of the relationship, they were not distressed or frustrated at his "coming." Many have said that they found the experience of watching the ejaculate spurt from his penis to be an exciting experience. Some women find the seminal fluid — in appearance, texture, odor, taste, and warmth — an erotic stimulus. We think that when two people love each other and show it, most of the so-called repulsive aspects of sexuality are, in fact, sources of pleasure, appreciation, and even comedy.

A final note on climax. Often you will move toward orgasm, either together or at different times. Couples in long-term relationships have a tendency to equate climax with conclusion. One of the most satisfying aspects of lovemaking can be the relaxation and closeness that follows an intense orgasm. It is in this time that you can experience the quality of your love together. After orgasm your body is still aroused and there is much pleasure yet to be experienced in the ensuing cuddling, caressing, or gentle kissing. It is during these times that you can experience the connection that transcends sex differences, by sharing your humanity, your vulnerability, and your sensual satisfactions.

The following activities are designed to help you and your partner increase your sexual pleasure by suggesting ways that you may not have thought of to be together sexually.

(a) Play an opposite role in bed for the next week. If you are normally passive, initiate things and be active. If you are usually active, try being passive in all aspects of your sexual encounters.

(b) Schedule two nights in one week for yourselves sexually. On the first night do what you can to please your mate; make sure you ask for ideas or instructions. On night two, you are the receiver of pleasure; remember to breathe and let yourself be touched and pleased.

(c) Spend one day "reversing" your sex. When you wake up in the morning, imagine in your body and mind that you are the opposite sex. Dress in your usual way, perform your daily routines but do them in word and deed the way you would expect someone of the opposite sex to do them. If you need some coaching, ask your partner. If you are a man and perceive women to be gentle, or standoffish, seductive, emotional, or subservient *be that way around both women and men*. If you are a woman and see men as aggressive, loud, crude, or controlling, *be that way*. Play the role all day and into the night, including in bed.

(d) One of you verbally complete one of the following fantasies to your partner:

I'm at a party. I'm very attracted to someone there. He is with a partner, as I am with you. I manage to touch him casually during conversation to watch the way he responds. I know that he is interested in me and I am really turned on. I....

There is a woman ahead of me in the hall of the motel. She reeks of money and the fragrance of expensive perfume. There is something regal about her. She has an aura of luxury, fine taste, and of having plenty of time. She looks directly into my eyes with the message that she is available to me. I....

(e) The next time you're making love, make an agreement with your partner to voice every thought that comes into your mind. Make sure you include the complimentary things as well as the criticisms or catty remarks.

ACTIVITY #44
ACHIEVING GREATER SEXUAL PLEASURE AND INTIMACY

Every study on sexuality in long-term marriages has shown that couples who can talk openly with each other about their sexual relationship have sex more often, experience more pleasure, and feel more love for each other.

Take turns completing the following sentences.

1. I think one way in which we are alike sexually is... _____

_____

2. I think that one way in which we are different sexually is that you seem to want

_____

... and I seem to want...._____

_____

3. Something I might gain by being more sexually self-disclosing is.... _____

_____

4. Something I think you might gain by being more sexually disclosing is...._____

_____

5. What I fear about becoming more intimate in our sexual relationship is.... _____

_____

_____

6. I could add to our sexual pleasure and intimacy by... (pick as many as you like)

_____ telling you what I enjoy and what I don't

_____ asking for what I want

_____ telling you what turns me on

_____ being more playful

_____ increasing my spontaneity

_____ telling you my sexual fantasies

_____ touching you more on a daily basis, both non-sensually as well as sensually

7. A time I really enjoyed sex with you was... _____

_____

_____

_____

_____

_____

9
WHEN AND HOW TO CHOOSE
A RELATIONSHIP COUNSELOR

How do you know that you need professional help? People most clearly experience the need for professional help in times of crisis. You may have a problem you cannot solve by yourself. You may feel tension and anxiety increase as the problem persists. You may feel depressed by your failure to resolve it. These symptoms then begin to interfere with your usual ability to function in your life. Your life can't go on as usual anymore. You are in crisis.

A crisis in relationship can be brought about by basic events that occur in life like birth, death, pregnancy, an affair, a promotion, a physical move, new wealth, or loss of a job by either partner. We define crisis in a relationship as a life event that causes one or both of the partners to completely change or question the way they see themselves, their relationship, and the world.

There are four kinds of crises. The first is the *external* crisis. This crisis comes from an external event that happens outside our control. We may have contributed to the events leading to the crisis but it is the event itself that precipitates the unexpected. Examples are a promotion, an affair, a money loss, or a job loss. The external crisis demands that we develop new ways of dealing with life. We don't have control over the crisis but we can determine how we are going to react.

The second kind of crisis we call *internal*. It comes from inside us and usually occurs when some form of emotional vulnerability within us reaches the breaking point. When this happens you just have to fill the emotional void that you are feeling. You may feel dissatisfied with yourself or lonely in your relationship. You may feel that you need to separate, to be alone to sort things out. You feel a pressure to act. You cannot go on in the same way. You may want to tell your partner that you don't like what is happening in your marriage and want it to change completely.

The third kind of crisis is what we call the *natural order* crisis. It arises as part of the natural order of life, as you pass from one stage of life to another: from youth to middle age (the mid-life crisis); from one stage of relationship to another. A natural order crisis can come about when one or both partners retire. It can happen with the birth of children or when children leave home. These movements can generate a crisis because the old assumptions about how the relationship will be carried out are changed.

The fourth kind of crisis we call *catastrophic* crisis. This is a sudden devastating event over which you have no control. All you can do is suffer through it and learn and grow from the awful situation. There is a finality to the event. This might come through the death of a child, a serious illness of you or your partner, your house burning down, or an accident involving the immediate family. It may come about through a miscarriage, murder, or the suicide of a loved one. In a catastrophic crisis you can no longer go back to the way things were; your life in some way has changed dramatically because of some event over which you have absolutely no control.

The experience of crisis brings the realization of your own limits in dealing with a particular difficulty and the need for outside help. Many people, however, deny that they need help, which can be a disaster for the relationship and may lead to another crisis. Recognizing when you can't solve a problem on your own is a sign of health and maturity. It means that you are willing to face reality.

Sometimes one or both partners in a relationship have less dramatic feelings of concern but are dissatisfied about the quality of their life together. In this case you may feel lonely, bored, or frustrated that your relationship is not more satisfying. You may not even be able to say why. Getting outside help can give you the opportunity to find the basis of your misgivings and get you on track again before you have a crisis later on.

A relationship that has a high degree of conflict — that is, one in which there is ongoing fighting without resolution — will continue to be full of conflict unless you find someone to intervene and teach you how to break this cycle. You will need help dealing with anger and conflict as part of solving your relationship problems. This kind of relating can be a habit and even have a certain comfort because it is familiar, but there are other ways that can be learned by anyone who wants something more from life.

If a couple has decided to separate and wants to do that constructively, a counselor can be useful as a way of making the transition. This kind of counseling is referred to as mediation counseling. The object is not to assist the couple to find ways of reconciling their differences so much as it is to help them negotiate the details of their separation or divorce.

In new relationships, where a couple is wanting to marry or make a more serious commitment to one another, counseling can do a great deal to enhance their relationship and to ensure its health and longevity. In this instance there is no history of bad experience together to interfere in the development of a satisfying relationship. Since most of us have never learned how to relate intimately to another, there are many benefits to be derived from discovering what relationships are about and developing the skills needed to have a satisfying relationship.

a. I'M NOT GOING TO SPILL MY GUTS TO A STRANGER

Most people, particularly men, are reluctant to go to a counselor. Both women and men frequently fear that they will be criticized, blamed for their partner's problems, or made to look stupid or wrong. These fears originate in our experiences as children when we were blamed or made to feel stupid and wrong for doing something our parents or teachers didn't like. We still carry the memory of those experiences with us and protect ourselves from further pain or embarrassment by avoiding any situation where that might re-occur. This is unfortunate and can get in the way of getting the help we need.

In our experience of counseling couples, some of the most reluctant participants get the most from counseling once they realize the counselor does not intend to make them feel bad or guilty about themselves. That doesn't mean you will like everything you hear. We all have things to learn about relationships and most of us have habits that prevent our being happy with our partners. You may have to change something to have a better life with your partner.

There are a number of erroneous ideas that most of us carry that prevent us from seeking help when we need it. The first of these is that anyone can make marriage or relationship work by using common sense; everyone knows how, you just have to do it. The second idea is that marriages/relationships are very private and personal and should never be discussed openly with other people. Third, only fools or incompetents need to learn how to be married or have a relationship. Fourth, if you really love each other, it will work. Or if you are having problems that you can't solve, you were not meant for each other. And last but not least, if you're having problems something is wrong. In other words marriage/relationship should be easy and problem-free.

We see conflict and difficulty as an inevitable part of any relationship that is alive and growing. These are not the real problems. The real problems are an unwillingness to learn something new, to acknowledge that you don't know how to do this on your own, and to learn how to handle conflict and differences in a constructive way.

b. CHOOSING A COUNSELOR

When looking for a counselor that will suit your needs there are several things to consider. The first is a practical consideration. How will the cost of counseling be covered? Fees range from $35 to $125 per hour, depending on the qualifications and experience of the counselor and the area in which he or she works. You need to find out what your medical insurance will cover. Coverage is usually restricted to psychiatrists and registered psychologists or other accredited professionals. If you are able and willing to pay for counseling personally your options will be much broader. There are many family and marriage/relationship counselors who do not fall into the group of "covered" professionals, but who are competent and experienced.

To find out who is doing this kind of work you need to do some research. If you have an employee assistance program where you work, they can tell you what resources are available in your area. Your family doctor may be able to suggest a number of resources. Each city also has central information directories for these and other services that can be accessed through the telephone directory or operator directory assistance. Friends who have had counseling may be aware of counseling resources that they can recommend.

Once you are aware of the available resources, you need to select the one that will be best for you. Sometimes this involves visiting several professionals before you make your decision. You need to decide ahead of time what you are looking for. Here are two things to consider:

(a) What credentials do you think this person should have in order for you to feel confident that they will be able to help you? How much and what kind of counseling experience should they have had?

(b) Who *is* he or she as a person? In order to be competent to help someone learn how to have a good relationship he or she must be capable of doing that personally. You can best judge this by how well this person relates to you, which can only be determined by firsthand experience.

One of the ways to find the answers to these questions is to call a prospective counselor and ask for an interview or consultation to get a feel for the counselor.

In our initial contact with a new couple we set up a consultation for half an hour, at no cost, as an opportunity for us to meet one another. It is also a chance for the couple to talk about what it is they want from counseling. We talk about what we do in working with couples and what they can expect. We also talk about the length of time we will work with them and the cost. The couple is encouraged to ask any questions about us that they have and to clear up any reservations they might have. If they decide in this time that they want to work with us then we set up a schedule of sessions. If they are undecided at the end of the consultation we end with an agreement that they will call if they do decide to work with us.

In choosing a counselor it is important that you have confidence in her or him as a person and as a professional. You must have confidence that you can be yourself and learn what you need to develop your relationship. You will both have to be satisfied with your choice. You may have to interview several people before finding the right one for you. Don't be discouraged; just consider this effort an indication that you want the best for your relationship. Most people know intuitively who will work well with them. There is usually a feeling of rapport with the counselor, even if you are afraid of being in his or her office. Actually experiencing some degree of fear or anxiety is good because it indicates that you are taking a risk and are investing in the outcome of the counseling.

c. WHAT IS THE COUNSELING PROCESS LIKE?

Most people come to counseling when they are in conflict. They probably have tried everything they know to solve the problems, but without success. The role of the counselor is to find out what problems they have and help them develop skills to resolve them. This usually will involve learning how to disclose openly and honestly, both positive and negative thoughts and feelings; learning to deal with anger constructively; and acquiring skills in handling conflict and in problem solving.

When a couple begins counseling in a state of conflict, they are often looking to the counselor for a quick cure. A competent counselor will not provide an immediate solution but will help the couple to develop the skills they need, while addressing their particular problems. When we are working with couples, our goal is to help them clarify their feelings, beliefs, and values rather than advise them on whether they should stay together or separate. No one can tell you whether your relationship will work or not; only you can decide.

We work with couples in a program we've designed that aims to provide a couple with knowledge about relationships, awareness of their attitudes about relationships, awareness of their behavior in relationships, and skills for effective relating. The program consists of twelve hours of counseling over a six- to nine-week period and combines two-hour sessions with the couple alternating with individual one-hour sessions. This gives each partner a chance to deal with his or her own issues that are separate from relationship issues, but that may have an impact on the relationship. People like this design because it has a defined beginning and end. At the end of the 12 hours the couple will not have solved all their problems but they will have learned some basic skills required to deal with them. They can then decide whether or not they want to continue the counseling. They are always free to return at any time if they get into a conflicted situation that they can't handle on their own.

d. PRIVATE COUNSELING VERSUS COUPLES WORKSHOPS

Private counseling and couples workshops offer different kinds of help and different opportunities. Private counseling affords individual attention to each partner. It offers both feedback and intervention by the counselor. This is particularly useful to couples who are in a high degree of conflict or crisis. Couples workshops allow you to step out of your regular routine and into a different setting to focus your attention on your relationship without any outside distractions. It gives you an opportunity to experience your partner in a different environment, in a different way. It allows time for reflection on your life and your relationship that you might otherwise not do. It also gives you an opportunity to know other couples who are interested in developing their relationship and struggling with difficulties.

The weakness in couples workshops may be in the structure or lack of structure of the workshop. For example, some workshops are set up in a retreat style where a couple may talk about their difficulties and the rest of the participants give feedback or suggestions to them. We think that this can be ineffective unless all the participants are well developed in their ability to see relationships clearly; most couples who attend workshops are not able to do that. A couple will only benefit from feedback that is accurate and nonjudgmental. Other couples groups are based on specific assumptions, such as marriage encounter groups that are religiously based and assume that marriages should last. Aside from these limitations, couples workshops that offer the opportunity to learn more about yourself in relationship and develop better relationship skills can be helpful in preventing destructive conflict and building more satisfying partnership.

We have worked out a structure for couples workshops that we think works well. Small workshops — usually eight to ten couples — are run as weekend retreats, structured to provide couples with privacy while they address their own difficulties. You talk only with your partner, although leaders are available during breaks for informal discussions. Private counseling sessions with the leaders are built into the format so that each couple has an opportunity to work on their own particular problems. Information is provided in the workshop in the form of short talks to teach people about relationships. These brief talks, plus experiential learning activities, help couples to discover how they interact in their relationship while learning skills that they can take home — skills such as self-disclosure, listening, anger management, conflict resolution, problem solving, and value clarification. Couples work toward understanding the importance of their intention and goodwill in their daily interactions. Couples examine the similarities and differences in their values and determine the kind of relationship they want to have. Some couples will decide whether they want to be together or not. Most of the couples who attend the workshops are in a fair degree of conflict and/or crisis, though some will be there for a "tune-up" because they feel they have lost the closeness they once had. Our experience over the last 15 years is that these workshops, as we conduct them, are far more effective than private counseling.

e. DIVORCE INSURANCE: THE IMPORTANCE OF PRE-MARITAL COUNSELING

In spite of the high divorce rate, couples continue to marry. In 1985, over two million couples tied the knot in North America. Marriage continues to be the most popular choice when women and men decide they want to formalize their commitment; 90% of the population marries at least once. One out of four marriages involves couples in which one or both have married before, but even these couples seldom take time to prepare for marriage the second time around. In the last five years many programs have been designed to prepare couples for marriage. The intention has been to prevent marriage problems before they start and, therefore, prevent divorce.

Do marriage preparation courses actually prevent divorce? A five-year study at the University of Toronto conducted by family medicine professor Edward Bader concluded that when couples who had taken marriage preparation ran into problems, they made a more positive, conscious effort to look for ways to solve the problem. Their relationships were dynamic and changing. Couples who did not have marriage preparation tended to have a negative, static attitude — deciding either to put up with the problems of the marriage or to get out. Couples who underwent marriage preparation reported decreasing conflict as their marriages progressed. In contrast, those unexposed to such courses showed patterns of conflict that were set early in the marriage and tended to continue. These latter couples also tended to have sexual problems related to the hostility in the relationship.

The problems a couple experiences during the engagement period will be carried into the marriage. They will also develop new problems as they adjust to each other and to married life. Unless they learn ways of effectively dealing with their current problems, they will continue to develop until they feel overwhelmed and unable to cope. Marriage preparation can prevent this. Working on learning conflict- and problem-solving skills is much easier for people in the early stages of a relationship because they feel so positive toward one another. It's a much more difficult task when people are in conflict and the problems have become serious.

Pre-marital counseling sets a pattern of taking time to develop your relationship. It recognizes the need for time and effort and encourages the possibility that the couple will continue to nurture their relationship as a process of growing together. For this reason the most beneficial courses involve sessions before the marriage and follow-up sessions after the marriage, usually within a year. This combination allows the couple to try out their skills in real life and later to get more help when the need for it is recognized.

There is a great deal to be said for the advantages of pre-marital counseling as part of ensuring a satisfying life together. To find out about marriage preparation courses contact your local church or family services association.